The Job-Ready Guide

The Job-Ready Guide

How to set yourself up
for career success

Anastasia de Waal

KoganPage

First published in Great Britain and the United States in 2019 by Kogan Page Limited

2nd Floor, 45 Gee Street
London
EC1V 3RS
United Kingdom
www.koganpage.com

122 W 27th St, 10th Floor
New York, NY 10001
USA

4737/23 Ansari Road
Daryaganj
New Delhi 110002
India

ISBNs

HARDBACK   978 0 7494 9847 4
PAPERBACK   978 0 7494 8325 8
E-ISBN   978 0 7494 8326 5

British Library Cataloguing-in-Publication Data

A CIP record for this book is available from the British Library.

Library of Congress Cataloging-in-Publication Data

Names: Waal, Anastasia de, author.
Title: The job-ready guide : how to set yourself up for career success /
    Anastasia de Waal.
Description: London ; New York : Kogan Page Limited, 2019. | Includes
    bibliographical references and index.
Identifiers: LCCN 2019004302 (print) | LCCN 2019007436 (ebook) | ISBN
    9780749483265 (Ebook) | ISBN 9780749498474 (hardback) | ISBN 9780749483258
    (paperback) | ISBN 9780749483265 (e-ISBN)
Subjects: LCSH: Vocational guidance. | Résumés (Employment) | Job hunting.
Classification: LCC HF5381 (ebook) | LCC HF5381 .W1525 2019 (print) | DDC
    650.1–dc23
LC record available at https://lccn.loc.gov/2019004302

Typeset by Integra Software Services, Pondicherry
Print production managed by Jellyfish
Printed and bound by CPI Group (UK) Ltd, Croydon CR0 4YY

CONTENTS

ABOUT THE AUTHOR

Anastasia de Waal is Director of the Family & Education Unit and Deputy Director of the think tank Civitas. She is also a qualified primary school teacher and founder of I Can Be, which takes disadvantaged primary school children to visit professionals in their workplaces. A regular contributor to the media, she is Chair of national family support charity Family Lives and Visiting Scholar at Cambridge University's Centre for Family Research.

Introduction

Are you a university or college student or are you a recent graduate? Whichever stage you're at in your studies, and whether you're pretty clear about your next move or you're feeling completely at sea career-wise, *The Job-Ready Guide* is here to help you navigate what you need to think about and what you need to do, to prepare yourself for the start of your working life.

> ## Any of these thoughts/questions sound familiar?
>
> 'I have literally no idea what job I want to do.'
>
> 'Can I get a job without having any work experience in the relevant industry?'
>
> 'Are you just supposed to pick up brochures at careers fairs?'
>
> 'Do I need to include my GCSE results on my CV?'
>
> 'What do I do if I don't know the answer to something during a job interview?'
>
> 'How do I know roughly what my starting salary should be?'
>
> 'What if I don't understand what I've been asked to do on my first day?'

Preparing for professional life

In today's highly competitive and increasingly complex job market, bolstering your employability as far as possible – from building up skills and experience, to understanding your target industry and cultivating professionalism – is more important than ever.

Over the course of the following chapters we'll develop and hone your career plan, working out where and what you're aiming for, and equipping you with the tools to get there. This book is angled primarily at those leaving university or college with a degree, but much of it can be readily applied to anyone embarking on their career.

Setting you up for career success is about preparing you both for the here and now – whatever stage of career planning you're currently at – and for your more long-term professional future. In other words, it's about building up your CV and your skills so that you can successfully apply and prepare for your first job after university or college, as well as working on the attributes you need to develop a strong record and reputation once you get into the workplace.

It's worth emphasizing from the start that career planning doesn't mean identifying and settling down into one type of job, or even industry, for the rest of your working life. Careers today are much more flexible, and the jobs that make up a successful career will often be very varied. Getting job-ready is about launching a professional life in which you're able to foster and seize opportunities, and continually progress – whatever form that progression may take.

What employers want you to know

Making the move from education to work can be daunting, and many soon-to-be employees say they feel underprepared for it. Significantly, many of your future bosses concur. Employers across industries, and line managers across levels of seniority, repeatedly complain about the same weaknesses in the candidates and new employees they see. As one employer puts it: 'New entrants to the job market are more educated than ever – a brilliant thing – but many of them are also less prepared for the demands of getting into and succeeding in working life.'

One of the main aims of writing this book was to contribute to correcting that disconnect between what employers want and what the workforce of the future has to offer by highlighting common pitfalls – and how to avoid them. Furthermore, my aim was to find out how you can equip yourself with the skills, experience and behaviours that are sought after by employers – to help you become a sought-after candidate. Key to this endeavour was to identify those 'in-between' aspects and soft skills; the often unspoken but crucial contributors to success in the workplace, or as one recent graduate put it, 'The things that employers expect, but no one tells you about.'

As a researcher by trade, I therefore set out to identify and pull together what employers want you to know about preparing for, getting into and excelling in the workplace. As well as gathering the views of those running organizations and those in charge of hiring on what they're looking for, I sought out 'warts and all' advice from different levels of professionals, across a spread of sectors. From recent graduates to senior executives, professionals with diverse backgrounds have revealed the strategies and tips *they* found helpful in establishing their careers, as well as what they wish they'd known or done differently. Students on the cusp of entering the workforce have also shared their experiences and what they've learnt so far. All quotes in the book have been anonymized, specifically to ensure the frankest feedback and most candid advice.

The Job-ready approach

Every suggested step in *The Job-Ready Guide* is simple and wholly achievable: none of the advice is rocket science – in fact it's mostly common sense – and all of it is straightforwardly applicable. The topics we'll look at will take you from the very beginnings of thinking about the industries you might be interested in, while you're still studying, to weighing up your options a year into your first job. In *The Job-Ready Guide* we'll work through:

Setting yourself up for success:

- What you can do during your studies to build up a strong CV.
- What to investigate to identify the career options most suited to you.
- How to plan, set up and get the most out of work experience placements.
- How to weigh up the value of doing further study in order to achieve your career goals.

Developing job-ready skills:

- The central characteristics of strong leadership and good teamwork in the workplace and how to develop the requisite skills.
- The key communication skills you need in the workplace and how to hone them for optimal effect.
- What problem-solving skills in the workplace entail, why employers want them and how to put them into practice.
- How to build a good understanding of your target industry and how to keep abreast of it as you progress in your career.

Looking for a job:

- How to organize yourself, and your background research, in order to optimize your job hunt.
- The attitude and habits to foster to be an effective professional.
- How to use social media to maximize your strength as a candidate.

- How to use networking to build up your exposure to job opportunities.
- Building up your money management skills and getting your finances in order.

Applying for a job:

- How to put together a strong and well-presented CV.
- What makes for powerful covering letters and how to complete application forms effectively.
- How to prepare for and perform as well as possible in job interviews.
- What to expect at assessment centre days, how to prepare for them and how to do your best in tasks.
- How to plan, prepare and deliver strong presentations.
- How to decide whether to accept a job offer, and how and when to try to negotiate a better deal.

Starting a job:

- What to think about and what to prepare to get off to a great start in a new job.
- What might come up on your first day in a job and how to get through it smoothly.
- How to build a good professional reputation and develop positive relationships in the workplace.
- When to start thinking about moving jobs and what you need to consider.

How to use the book

Each chapter of this guide will help you to build up the knowledge and understanding you need for each stage of the career development process, going on to look at how to practically implement the action you need to take. At the end of each chapter, a short exercise will help you to recap on core points covered and to reflect on how you can apply what we've discussed. As you go through the guide, keep in mind that there is rarely, if ever, only one 'correct' way of doing things in the context of preparing for the workplace. From how you format your CV to the questions you ask in an interview, these are ultimately your decisions to make and your journey will be unique. What you'll find in here is a roadmap to help you navigate your way on that journey.

How you read *The Job-Ready Guide* is up to you. You can approach the book by reading it through from start to finish, or alternatively by homing in on chapters that cover the specific topics you want guidance on. Whichever approach you decide to take, and wherever you've got to in your planning for the future, here's to getting Job-Ready!

A note on terminology

Throughout the book we've opted to use 'organization' as a catch-all term for any workplace, be it a business, charity, public service provider or educational establishment. The word 'industry' is used to describe an area of work and used interchangeably with the word 'sector'.

Part One
Setting yourself up for success

01
CV building

CV building is about identifying and honing transferable skills, maximizing what you can get out of your studies and seeking out additional opportunities to build up the attributes valued by employers.

It's never too early to be building up a strong CV, and in this chapter we'll be looking at how to get ahead of the game before you get to the point of applying for jobs. We'll work through 10 basic steps that you can implement while you're still studying, showing you how they pave the way for putting together a strong CV. If you're reading this at the end of your studies, and you *are* at the point of applying for jobs, don't worry: there is still plenty you can do to shore up your best possible CV. Going through the suggestions on how to strengthen your profile will help you to draw out relevant skills and experience, and present your record as effectively as possible.

We'll look at the specifics of how to compile and format the CV you submit to employers in Chapter 14. Our focus in this chapter is on what makes for, and how to prepare, persuasive 'material' to build a strong CV.

Linking your studies and wider experiences to your future – and potential – in the workplace lies at the heart of CV building. When we talk about strengthening your CV, therefore, we're talking about building up the skills and experience that will help you to succeed once you get into the industry you choose. In other words, CV building isn't a superficial exercise about what you can put down on paper, and it isn't even simply about coming up with content that will get your CV to the top of an employer's pile. Building a strong CV is about strengthening you as a candidate by identifying, fostering and making the most of opportunities and preparing you for a successful transition to the workplace.

Planning your CV: an overview

Let's start by imagining that your dream job has come up, and the employer is about to go through your CV. The basic elements your CV will cover are:

- your education and qualifications;
- your workplace experience (including paid, voluntary and unpaid work experience);
- information on your referees.

You'll also likely include references to:

- skills;
- achievements;
- extracurricular activities/interests.

With these categories in mind, what could you include that would make you a strong candidate? Over the course of the chapter we'll look at how to prepare for exactly that: what you can do to bolster your employability. In summary, you'll need to:

- build a strong track record on your course;
- make the most of wider opportunities on offer at your university/college;
- seek, research and implement careers advice, from career advisers, tutors/ lecturers and industry insiders;
- plan for and organize useful work experience opportunities;
- recognize and maximize the transferability of skills you are able to gain through part-time/vacation work and volunteering.

So, let's now look at how to go about boosting your opportunities and employability, practically, by applying 10 simple steps during your studies.

1 Sketch out a draft CV and treat it as a work in progress

You'll most likely have at least a basic form of CV, used, for example, to apply for part-time and vacation jobs. If you haven't, taking the main CV categories outlined above, sketch out your own first draft. Treat your draft CV as a running log of the achievements, skills and experiences you gain, including everything from grades to extracurricular activities, regularly reviewing what you can add to it. The key at this stage is to simply get down all relevant information, rather than making decisions about how best to present it and what to leave out. When it comes to polishing up and perfecting your CV, you'll have done a lot of the legwork in terms of thinking about what could go into it and will be able to focus on editing your content. Adding to your CV categories as you progress through your course won't only help you to include everything potentially relevant; it will also help you to firmly establish a workplace-facing mindset, embedding the link between what you are doing now and your future career prospects.

2 Apply professionalism to how you approach your studies

Don't wait until you get into the workplace to think about and implement professional habits and behaviours: start now. As well as being good practice for the future, you'll reap the benefits right away.

- **Take all your commitments seriously.** Make going to all your lectures and classes non-negotiable; don't sign up to events/societies/extra courses you probably won't go to.

- **Meet all your deadlines.** Plan in enough time to complete your work and don't leave it until the last minute to submit it; get library books back on time and avoid racking up fines.

- **Aim to produce high quality work.** From fully answering the specific essay question you've been set using the recommended reading, to practising your class presentation and thoroughly proofreading your essays, set yourself high standards and stick to them.

- **Be punctual.** Whether it's a lecture, tutorial meeting or work experience, make it a priority to turn up on time.

- **Work effectively with others.** From pulling your weight in group work to debating respectfully with your course mates, make your interactions with others as constructive and valuable as possible.

- **Keep yourself informed.** Read/watch/listen to the news daily and engage in the world around you rather than studying and living in a bubble.

- **Set clear boundaries between your studies and personal life.** Don't allow your social life to negatively impact on your work; be careful with your money so that, where possible, managing financial problems doesn't distract you from your studies.

3 Prioritize your studies and maximize what you get out of them

The single most important thing you can do when building up your CV is to do your best in your studies. Whatever you're studying, and regardless of the type of course you are doing, how you perform is going to be one of the central factors that employers judge you on. You therefore need to ensure that while broadening your experience, you don't lose sight of the fact that your studies must always be your priority, particularly time-wise. No number of impressive work experience placements or extracurricular achievements will trump a strong and consistent performance on your course.

As well as putting in the necessary time, aim high in your studies; for example, find out about course, departmental and college/university-wide awards and prizes – and have a go. Employers will be interested in exceptional performance, but even more importantly it can be very helpful to have goals to aim for as a way to motivate yourself. Aim to maximize what you are getting out of your course, however, rather than doggedly chasing achievement for the sake of it. An outstanding grade is valuable but even more so is the process of how you achieved it – the development of your learning, knowledge and skills.

With this point in mind, also set your own benchmarks to hit, such as mastering aspects of your course that you're struggling with, rather than writing them off. Aiming high isn't just about trying to perform your best, it's also about identifying your weaknesses and working on them. Success in this scenario may be finally understanding an aspect of your course, and not giving up on it until you do, rather than excelling in it. Balance identifying and working on your weaknesses with identifying your strengths and playing to them. For example, if you perform better in coursework than you do in exams, where possible tailor your module selections accordingly, and try to maximize your attainment in these courses with a view to bolstering your overall performance.

4 Capitalize on all available resources

Enhance the value you get from your studies by making the most of the resources you have available. Fully utilize university/college facilities on offer that will help your studies, whether it's the well-stocked library, readily available software or free access to industry-grade equipment and materials.

Engage with your lecturers and tutors. Join in after-class discussions with them; find out about their research or industry interests and follow their work; ask them to suggest extra reading or exercises when you are finding an aspect of the course difficult. As well as enhancing your learning experience and helping you to get more out of the course, having a rapport with your tutors and lecturers will be useful when it comes to moving on from your studies. Whether it's asking for their advice on the value of doing further study or their recommendations on where to apply for funding or, crucially, whether they would be prepared to be a referee for a job application, previously established links can be very valuable.

5 Make the most of the extracurricular offers at your university/college

There are likely to be many opportunities on offer at your university or college that could be very useful, skills and experience-wise, as well as enjoyable. These will include opportunities to gain experience that is directly relevant to your target industry, for example on the university newspaper if you are interested in journalism, or with a political society if you think you might want to go into politics. They'll also include wider opportunities that can help you to cultivate a broad range of skills and experience. Here are some typical examples:

- **Sports teams.** On top of gaining specific sporting skills, joining a team or sports club can give you opportunities to build teamwork skills, compete and even win prizes. There may also be ways to develop leadership and organizational experience, for example in captaining or training a team.

- **Societies.** Educational institutions tend to host a great variety of societies, where opportunities will range from becoming more informed about a particular subject area to developing a skill (for example, debating). There will also be chances to build up a broad spectrum of skills, from organizing events and fundraising, to building society membership and managing a society's budget, to networking within and outside the university or college.

- **Courses.** Universities and colleges often offer free or heavily subsidized courses, enabling you to build up your skill set, be it learning a language or coding.

- **Student leadership.** Whether it's getting involved in running the students' union or becoming a student representative on an institutional or departmental committee, getting involved in decision-making processes offers the chance to gain valuable experience and skills, work with professionals and effect change.

6 Recognize the added potential value of social opportunities

Socializing at university or college needn't only be about having fun and finding people you have something in common with. There's also unparalleled scope to broaden your horizons and build up future networks across sectors as well as within industries you're interested in. Make the most of the opportunities universities and colleges provide by being open to engaging with people across different subject areas and specialisms, not just within your own. Similarly, don't shy away from fostering a close-knit group of friends, but do avoid spending all your free time in a bubble made up of one set of people.

7 Use the careers service effectively

Many university and college careers advisers complain that students only make use of what they have on offer towards the end of their studies, when it's time to get a job. As one careers adviser puts it, too many students appear to only start thinking about their career and getting a job just before they graduate.

To make the best use of the careers advice service, find out what's available as soon as you start your course, and sign up to as many careers events as possible. See the opportunities available as training and preparation for the future. Even though you aren't yet applying for jobs, attend talks, go to on-campus careers fairs (even for sectors you're not targeting) and go to any advice surgeries on offer. Be open-minded when you are exploring your options, listening carefully to the advice that you get from different quarters. However, bear in mind that the information you are getting is to help you make your own decisions, so equally don't feel compelled to take a prescribed route or course of action. Furthermore, you will sometimes receive conflicting advice, so apply any guidance you get to your own specific circumstances and weigh it up critically. The sooner you start thinking about your employability and preparing for your future, the more chance you will have to make use of the advice and training you pick up and the clearer you will be about the options available.

8 Plan ahead and organize a number of work experience placements

It's worth organizing work experience opportunities at the earliest possible point. As well as enabling you to build up experience helpful to future applications, work experience is generally the only way to be able to gain first-hand insight into the realities of a job. The advantage of setting up work experience as early as possible, therefore, is that this will allow you time to explore different jobs and even sectors before settling on your preferred target. Work experience placements can also be very helpful in building industry networks and garnering insider advice, and can even lead to job opportunities, as we'll discuss in Chapter 3. A practical approach to arranging work experience is to use your first year of university/college to explore your options by doing several short stints (no more than a week) in a number of different workplaces. As you narrow down the field and jobs you're interested in, you can hone the focus of your placements the closer you get to finishing your course.

9 Maximize the benefits of any paid work you do

Your reason for doing paid work, be it a part-time job during your course or work over the vacation periods, will most likely be financial. There's also excellent potential within part-time paid work, however, for building up transferable skills and experience, and demonstrating that you have the attributes employers are looking for. For these reasons, as long as the time commitment involved in doing part-time work doesn't impinge on your studies, having a paid job while you study can be very valuable for your CV. Let's take an example of a part-time job a full-time student might have – working as a retail assistant – and look at how this can translate into strong CV material.

Examples of transferable skills and experience developed in a part-time retail job:

- **Working well under pressure.** Delivering good service at peak times eg on Saturdays and in the build up to Christmas.
- **Communication skills.** Following instructions from line managers, being informed about and answering customer questions about products, promoting products effectively.
- **Dealing with the public.** Handling difficult customers, serving several customers at once, satisfying customers' requirements.
- **Teamwork.** Working effectively with colleagues.
- **Organizational skills/time management.** Successfully combining full-time studies with part-time work.

Notably, in this example, although the skills outlined are developed in a part-time retail context, they can be applied across many industries, job descriptions and levels of seniority.

TIP: *A great place to start when looking for part-time paid work is your university/college. Some roles, such as research assistance work or lab technician support, may actually aid your studies and give you relevant industry experience. For other types of jobs, such as front of house or bar work, the location will be convenient, and the shifts will often fit well into student schedules.*

10 Highlight the value of voluntary work

Voluntary work, where you are offering your time to a charity or cause for free, can add value to your CV for several reasons. Firstly, voluntary work can demonstrate your dedication to a particular issue. This can provide insight into your values and priorities, as well as your understanding of a cause; this in turn may link to an industry you are keen to get into. For example, if you're interested in getting into teaching, voluntary work with children or young people can help to build up your credentials. Furthermore, voluntary work may be a way to gain experience within your targeted field. Taking teaching as an example again, volunteering to be a reading partner with primary school children each week will give you experience of working in a school. Depending on the nature of the work you are doing, volunteering can also build up valuable transferable skills, from communication to fundraising skills.

Transferable skills

Here are a few more examples of transferable skills you will likely have gained through your studies, extracurricular activities and/or part-time paid work:

- problem-solving;
- decision-making;
- research skills;
- negotiation;
- leadership;
- networking;
- project management.

What I found useful:

'While joining societies can do a lot to build up a CV, I actually didn't find the societies I joined at my university particularly stimulating. I did, however, really enjoy going to events, which led me to join two events' committees myself. I personally found organizing events more enjoyable than being involved in subject-specific societies, and I have often used the experiences that I have had as part of those committees in competency-based interviews.'

What I wish I'd known:

'I wish I'd had a better understanding of how to get the most out of my degree. Tutors and lecturers offer office hours for a reason – it's important to utilize all the resources available to you, as I often struggled to understand difficult concepts through reading alone.'

O.R. (Final year university student)

Exercise

Think of a paid part-time job you've had. Going through the day-to-day tasks it involved, outline the transferable skills that you developed that would be valuable in an industry you're interested in. Now do the same for any voluntary work you've been involved in, be it a one-off or regular commitment: can you identify skills you could apply to an industry you might target?

02
Career planning

Fully exploring your career options is critical to making informed choices. Not everyone reading this will be doing a course with a clearly mapped-out route ahead, such as medicine or law, or even an 'aligned' course, such as a finance degree regarded as suitable preparation for a career in the City. Many of you will be doing, or have just finished, a course that could potentially lead to numerous, different career paths. Furthermore, in cases where your course *does* link to or align with a specific job or industry, there will still be options to navigate, from specialisms to necessary further study – as well as the bigger question of whether you really *are* on the right path for a happy and successful future.

Career planning is also crucial for writing effective job applications: the greater your understanding of what a job entails, and therefore the more compelling your reasons for applying for it, the more likely you are to be successful.

In this chapter, we'll look at how to set about investigating your options: by navigating the information available about what's out there, showing you how to explore your choices and working out what type of work would suit you best.

But before we go any further, a note of caution. The aim of career planning is *not* to identify a career you must then sign up to for life. Instead, it's about launching a successful and fulfilling working life that in many cases will end up being made up of a series of jobs, either in one industry or possibly in several. Career progression is about moving forward professionally but not necessarily in one direction and therefore not necessarily in one industry. For this reason, we'll talk about 'careers' and 'jobs' interchangeably. The first job you have will therefore contribute to, but not dictate, the rest of your working life, so don't put yourself under undue pressure to get things 'perfectly right' at the outset. A good way to think about your first job after studying is as the first building block of your professional life.

Your basic educational profile

Your first, very simple, task when you set about career planning is to jot down your basic educational profile: the focus and format of your studies and overall outcome. The purpose of doing this is to set up your own 'filters' (like search engine filters) for when you are investigating which jobs you are eligible for. For example, some careers will require specific postgraduate training. Similarly, some jobs will require a particular degree subject or a specific type of degree – such as a Bachelor of Science (BSc). Two important caveats are worth highlighting at this point, however. Firstly, the aim of setting up your 'filters' isn't to circumscribe your options, it's to work out what they *currently* are: further study opportunities, for example, may enable you to enter professions you aren't presently eligible for. Secondly, keep in mind that for many graduate jobs, employers will be more interested in the fact that you have a degree – through which you've built up transferable skills – than the specific subject you studied.

Performance on your course is also a key part of your vital educational stats; for some graduate jobs, employers may be more interested in how well you have done in your course than, again, they are in what the course subject was. Some graduate jobs, for example, will require a minimum degree classification: a 2:1 is a common minimum entry requirement for a number of jobs. Even when the specific knowledge or skills you learned during your course are not directly applicable to a job, course performance matters because employers often use it to gauge how well you have developed transferable skills – from analytical skills to communication skills. Employers will also often look at your course performance as an indication of your work ethic, how well you are able to apply yourself to projects and tasks, and your broader abilities. A further note to add is that in some cases your previous educational qualifications will be part of the entry criteria for some career paths. Examples include certain routes into teaching, where a minimum C grade or equivalent at GCSE is required in English and maths.

Your basic educational profile, therefore, could look something like this:

Humanities BA (History) graduate with a 2:1.

If you haven't finished your course, use your predicted outcome, based on your results so far.

Let's now do a test run of your basic educational profile against two or three jobs you are interested in. These can be within one industry or across industries. Go online and find a job advertisement for each of these jobs (eg on milkround.com): you may well not have the necessary work experience for the posts, but do you currently, or are you on course to, have the educational qualifications required?

Researching your career options

Exploring your career options is ultimately a research project, in which your research question is 'What job am I suited to?' based on your interests and priorities and educational background.

The initial part of the research process is about exploring the range of jobs you could do with your current educational background. The second part of the process is about matching up your priorities – your interests, values and what motivates you – with the jobs available to you. This part of the research process may also entail exploring further study options that will enable you to pursue a particular career path. The final part of the research process is about testing out your choices by getting hands-on insight through work experience.

Finding out about what you could do

When it comes to familiarizing yourself with the jobs you can apply for, by far the most useful resource is your university or college's careers service. It's all too easy to forget that you have access to a service *specifically* designed to help you explore your options and plan your career, right there on your doorstep.

The help you can get from your careers service will range from practical training, for example, on how to perform well in job interviews, to one-to-one tailored advice clinics, to guidance on where to find relevant information. When you're trying to work out which careers would suit you, a one-to-one appointment with a careers adviser to go through your educational background and interests is a good way to start. At this stage you want to build up a bank of ideas about areas of work that you are eligible for, with a view to then working out how they fit in with your interests and what you would enjoy doing day-to-day. Again, you may also look at how further study opportunities relate to jobs of interest. A careers adviser can help guide you through your options by helping you to get to grips with the opportunities on offer using examples of job profiles and probing your priorities through questioning and tools such as online tests.

The more you know about the jobs that make up the labour market, the more chance you have of setting off on a career path that will really suit you. Recent research has found that half of university graduates have no plan about what they are going to do next. To paraphrase a graduate recruitment consultant on the subject, such high levels of uncertainty among graduates comes down to a combination of lack of thought about the future during their studies and lack of awareness about the jobs that make up the labour market. This lack of awareness is a complaint from employers more widely, who often criticize what they see as a disconnect between education and the workforce. As one employer puts it, 'Students just don't seem to be getting properly informed about the jobs that are out there.' University and college careers advisers, in turn, often complain about how difficult it is to get students to use their services – leading them to resort to tactics such as holding careers advice sessions in the bar in a bid to woo take-up! Make it your aim not to fall into this trap and, instead, get up to speed with what the labour market currently looks like. Your careers service will have a library of resources, generally in both hard copy and online, but also look further afield, bearing in mind that technological developments result in the emergence of a steady stream of new jobs. Do your own research legwork, including looking at job descriptions on job sites and investigating careers guidance resources at your local public library. There are lots of helpful resources and books out there, such as Lucy Tobin's *The Book of Jobs* (published by Hachette UK), outlining the details of what different jobs entail, their earning potential and their entry requirements.

> **TIP:** *Whether you've finished your course or not, it's worth having a chat with a recruitment consultant. Recruitment agencies tend to be keen to get strong talent on their radar, if not yet on their books, and can be a really useful source of ideas as to the types of jobs you might be suitable for.*

Talk to course alumni about their career paths...

Your university/college careers service may also be able to put you in touch with former students, giving you the opportunity to find out about their career paths. This is especially helpful if you have the chance to speak to past students who did the same course as you. How did they identify their available options, and what did they do to get their career started? Most careers services also hold cases studies on file outlining the career paths pursued by previous students. Many educational institutions also have dynamic alumni networks, again offering opportunities to quiz people who did your course, or one in a similar field, and are now in employment. If you do get a chance to speak to past students, as well as asking them about how they got their career going, ask them about opportunities they feel they missed and what they might do differently with the benefit of hindsight. It's also really worth asking whether they enjoy their current work, and if not, why, as well as whether they have any plans to move into a job or industry they think they'd prefer.

... And to professionals more widely

Don't limit yourself to talking to alumni from your university/college: widen the net. Talking to professionals at different stages in their careers, with different starting points, is a great way to pick up valuable advice. One approach is to look for people in an industry you are interested in and ask them to talk you through how they got where they are, from when and how they identified that they wanted to work in that industry to how they entered it. Work experience placements can provide an opportune chance to do this. It's also worth talking to people across industries – drawing on contacts from your neighbours to family friends (we'll talk more about using personal networks in Chapter 12). Looking at other people's careers and talking to them about the choices they made is a really useful way to gain ideas. Especially useful is to speak to people you know who really *enjoy* their jobs, to find out how – and when – they identified a career path that suited them so well.

Your priorities: what motivates you?

Looking for a job that you find rewarding, stimulating and that reflects your values might sound like a bit of a luxury. But it really matters that you prioritize finding a job that, as far as possible, fulfils these aims. Bear in mind that you will be spending up to eight hours a day, five days a week working. Invariably, we'll all find ourselves at times not loving a job we have – but the more thought and time you invest in working out what would suit you, the less likely you are to find yourself regretting particular choices. Furthermore, a fulfilling job isn't just about being happier at work. The more motivated you are by your job the better an employee you will be, and the more successful.

Identifying your priorities is about narrowing down your options to cater for your personality, your values, your interests and the aspects of a job you would enjoy. Right at the heart of your priorities sits a single question: what motivates you?

Below is a list of commonly held priorities; rank the ones that are important to you in order and cross out the ones that aren't:

- high salary;
- helping people;
- getting to travel abroad;
- working outdoors;
- having a hands-on role;
- working with people;
- working independently;
- working in an organization that shares your values;
- flexibility;
- variety;
- prestige/future prestige;
- leading and managing other people;
- doing a variety of tasks;
- working for a good cause.

Now think about whether there are other priorities, not listed above, that matter to you. If there are, add them in and redo your rankings. What top three priorities have you ended up with?

With these top three priorities in mind, let's now think about how they match up to different jobs. Returning to some of the jobs you are interested in, from what you know about them so far, do your priorities feature in these roles? Does one job of interest match your priorities better than others?

What would work for you?

As well as thinking about your priorities, you need to think about your skills, your strengths and your weaknesses. Below is a list of 17 well-known jobs. The aim of the exercise we're about to do is to help you further explore which elements of a job would suit you, bringing together what motivates you with what you enjoy and the skills you have. It's also useful for your careers research to get into the mindset of thinking about the details of what particular jobs entail. For example, what do you know about the skills a police officer requires, and what activities do you think make up a politician's workload?

Rank the following occupations, identifying (a) what you would like about the job or **not** like about the job, and (b) whether you think you currently have the necessary skills and educational background:

- teacher;
- accountant;
- mechanic;
- lawyer;
- computer software developer;
- small business owner;
- fire fighter;
- politician;
- farmer;
- author;
- fashion designer;
- chef;
- journalist;
- police officer;
- graphic designer;
- doctor;
- theatre director.

Looking at your ranking of these occupations, how do your preferences fit with your top three identified priorities? Do they feature any or all of your priorities?

It's worth highlighting that we're deliberately looking at jobs where in some cases you *won't* have the necessary qualifications. The goal is to identify which elements in a job appeal to you, and it's always worth keeping your mind open to jobs that further education could enable you to do.

The aim of this type of exercise is to start to build a picture of what you are looking for, in order to further hone it. Add to these by trying out an online career planning tool, such as Prospects.ac.uk's 'Career Planner', to help you to keep piecing together information about which jobs might suit you. As with all careers' guidance, keep in mind that you should use online career planning tools as suggestions to help inform your decisions, rather than prescriptions.

Honing your options through work experience

In the next chapter we'll look in detail at how to go about organizing work experience and how to get the most out of it. One of the main benefits of gaining work experience is to get experience itself under your belt, as well as industry knowledge and contacts, all of which will help to strengthen your job applications and set you up well for the workplace. The other key benefit of work experience is that it gives you the chance to see what jobs are really like, which is an essential part of informed career planning. In order to identify what you will choose to focus your job applications on, you need to get as much first-hand insight and understanding as possible about the jobs you're interested in. This practical exploration is about whittling down your options and will help you to choose between different industries, as well as identify which particular part of an industry you want to target. Furthermore, speaking to people working in an industry, seeking honest accounts of the pros and cons, is as invaluable for your career planning research as experiencing the industry yourself.

What I found useful:

'Talking to people and exploring the different routes into the area in which I was interested was incredibly useful. I lacked confidence and believed that I would need to have this experience or have studied that particular degree to be able to get a job in luxury fashion management. It was only after I spoke to many people who worked in the industry that it became apparent that there wasn't just one "right" way in. Once I started talking to people it really got me motivated and helped boost my confidence.'

What I wish I'd known:

'I wish I had made better use of the careers service and really thinking deeply about what I wanted to do before my degree finished. The majority of my peers were going into finance and banking roles, which I definitely knew I didn't want to do. I had enjoyed studying for my history degree so I applied for a Master's straight after I completed my undergraduate course. I did end up finally working in a career that I loved, but with hindsight the route I took could have been more direct had I given my options after my undergraduate degree more careful consideration earlier on rather than jumping into a Master's in a bid to be doing something!'

I.V.-H. (Fashion and luxury business consultant)

Exercise

Think back to your career aspirations when you were a child. What did you want to be when you were 5 years old, 10 years old and 15 years old? What factors determined your aspirations at each stage, silly or serious, and did each aspiration differ a lot? If you can't recall any particular career aspirations as a child, can you recall when you first thought about your future career?

Now think about your current career planning and whether there is any overlap between the priorities and interests of your younger self and those you have today.

03
Work experience and internships

Before we go any further, a note on terminology. In this chapter we're looking at work experience that you organize yourself within industries you are considering applying to, and that you undertake outside your course programme. We'll use the term 'work experience' to refer to short periods of time spent in a workplace, often shadowing people as they do their work. We'll use the term 'internships' to refer to longer periods of time spent in a workplace, often during the summer. 'Placements' is another term that is sometimes used to refer to work experience, but this term is generally used to describe set periods of work experience that are an essential part of a course or module. It's worth noting, however, that some organizations use the terms placements and internships interchangeably.

Work experience and internships both provide an invaluable opportunity: immersion in the working world. A common complaint from employers is that graduates don't move easily enough from study to the workplace. They list weaknesses such as a lack of awareness about basic working life protocols (turning up on time, meeting deadlines, behaving professionally), and there really is no better way of getting well versed in what to do in the workplace than seeing it and practising it yourself.

Work experience vs internships

The key difference between work experience and internships is how long they last, which in turn defines their focus. While work experience could entail just a day of shadowing and doesn't tend to last more than two weeks, internships are generally longer and can range from a month to even a year. The other difference is their purpose. Work experience tends to be more about getting to see what happens in a workplace, whereas internships tend to be about actually trying out the work. Finally, work experience is usually unpaid, whereas an increasing number of internships today are (modestly) waged.

Timings

Whether you're setting up a few days' work experience or an internship, allow plenty of lead-in time to organize it. Internships in particular can be highly competitive, especially when they are paid. You also need to make sure that you plan the time you will have available to gain workplace experience carefully. For example, it can be useful to dip your toe into an industry by doing a week's work experience, to help you decide whether or not to apply for a summer internship in it.

Funding unpaid work experience and internships

A key consideration when trying to gain unpaid experience is whether you can afford to. If you're studying and you do a short work experience stint locally, particularly part-time, money will be less of an issue. Things can start to get difficult when you have to forfeit paid work, say a summer job, and/or when an unpaid internship or work experience isn't local and you need to pay for travel to get there.

We'll talk a bit more about combining paid work with unpaid work experience later, but the first thing to do when planning work experience and internships is to figure out what is practically available to you. When are you free, where can you stay if it's not local, what are your travel options and what access do you have to funds (earnings, savings or external funding)? Doing this will allow you to see whether you can afford to do unpaid work experience, for example, by living with family/friends and surviving financially on savings. It will also allow you to identify any funding opportunities you could apply for. Many universities and colleges have bursaries to help students undertake unpaid work experience, generally for summer internships. Not surprisingly, these tend to be highly sought after, so once again giving yourself a good lead-in time will allow you to get in a strong application.

Work experience

The main purpose of work experience is to get to see what happens in the workplace. You might end up doing a range of different things, and you might alternate between observing other people working and doing small bits of work yourself. Because work experience is often more informal, there can be more of a chance for you to decide what you want to get out of it.

So, for example, do you want to spend time in a workplace getting familiar with a range of different jobs? Or is your aim to closely shadow one particular role? Be specific about what you're hoping to get out of work experience when you're arranging it. This is essential to making sure your experience isn't disappointing. If you're clear about what you want to achieve when you approach an employer, that will help them decide whether they can accommodate you. Simply *being* in a workplace for a period is not necessarily valuable. Sitting in front of a computer, left largely to your own devices, for example, is not ideal (or unheard of).

Setting up work experience

One of the good things about arranging short work experience placements is that there is much more scope for flexibility – both on timings and length. For example, you might be able to set up a week's work experience over a month, going in for a day a week. Or if you're working in a vacation job to earn money, you might be able to arrange a few days off to do work experience. Because work experience periods can be short, another thing to consider is setting up multiple work experience placements so that you can get to see a variety of jobs, or even different industries.

When, where and whom to approach

The comparatively informal nature of work experience means that although there doesn't tend to be a straightforward application process, there is little limit to where you can approach. So, where to start?

1 Work out your timings: when and how long can you do work experience for?

2 Draw up a list of specific jobs, within one industry or more, that you would most like to see.

3 Put together a list of work experience options, by taking a three-part approach:

   a A useful first step is to think about whether you have any personal connections. Does a family friend or neighbour work in an industry of interest to you? They themselves might not be able to offer you work experience, but they may well be able to connect you to someone who can.

b Find out what your university/college's careers service can offer in terms of helping you to organize work experience.

c The next port of call is to approach organizations directly. Not many organizations advertise work experience, so you will likely need to 'cold call' them. The more targeted your work experience request, the less likely it is to disappear into an administrative black hole. Many workplaces list individual email addresses on their websites, but if that fails you can always try making contact via social media. Be brief and be clear about why you want to do work experience with that particular organization in any requests you make. If you are contacting an organization via social media, condense your request into one line, eg: 'I am a [*fill in the gap*] and would be very keen to do work experience with you if possible: may I contact you via email? Many thanks [*Name*]'. If you get a positive initial response from an organization, write back to them as soon as possible, outlining what you are currently doing, why you would like to do work experience with them and your availability.

Doing work experience

Employers have been known to forget that work experience placements have been arranged, so do drop them a line the week before, saying how much you are looking forward to joining them and reiterating your agreed starting date. As with starting a new job, follow some first week rules (see Chapter 20): err on the side of a smart dress code, make sure you know where you're going and make sure you've established an arrival time with the workplace.

Although it can be daunting not only being new but being in a workplace temporarily, it's worth joining in with workplace life as much as possible. This will allow you to see and try a greater variety of things. Meeting and interacting with people more will also help you to practise the communication skills that are so vital to a successful working life.

It's worth keeping in mind that, at least in some cases, work experience is seen as doing you a favour. Opportunities may arise to help out, but when you are shadowing work and are there for only a few days, you, rather than the organization, will tend to be benefiting. So be as accommodating as possible – and make yourself useful where possible – and try not to be too needy. Don't forget that everyone there has their normal workload to do, and keeping you occupied is an extra task.

Internships

There is a good deal of overlap between internships and work experience, but a common differentiator is that an internship more often involves getting to *do* work rather than shadowing other people doing theirs. Another difference is that the length of time you spend in a workplace will affect your role within the organization. Someone who joins the workplace for a month or more, and in many cases is paid, is likely to be treated more like an employee. And it's these two differences that make for one of the most valuable things about doing an internship: the opportunity to test out a job – and workplace.

Given the longer time commitment, it's important that you only apply for internships when you're really interested in the industry. You're investing yourself for an extended period, so you need to make sure it's a worthwhile opportunity.

Applying for internships

It's increasingly common for internship advertisements to look like standard job advertisements. You'll generally find them on an organization's website, as well as sometimes on recruitment sites, such as Prospects.ac.uk. The application process also frequently mirrors that of job applications. Internship candidates might be asked to write a covering letter and/or complete an application form outlining their suitability for an internship, referencing their achievements and educational background, and how their career plans link with where they are applying. You can apply the same tips when applying for internships as you do for job applications (see Chapter 15).

Affording an internship

Earlier in the chapter we discussed the fact that some internships are paid while others aren't, as well as funding opportunities available from universities and colleges. Many organizations that offer internships now pay at least a small wage, such as the minimum wage, while some charities, for example, still offer unpaid internships. If you are taking an unpaid internship, do make sure that you find out if there are any other subsidies; for example, some organizations will offer a daily allowance for lunch and/or travel costs. It's also always worth asking if there is scope for flexibility. Being able to intern part-time, for example, or finish earlier each day to accommodate paid work, is a request many employers will be prepared to accommodate. If travel costs are affected by peak-time tickets, asking to start each day an hour later to reduce your ticket price is also something to consider.

Starting an internship

You'll feel a lot more confident about your first day if you've set yourself up well. Again, apply the 'first week at work' tips in Chapter 20 to make sure that you start off smoothly, equipped with the necessary information and practicalities. Treat your internship like a job, whether it's paid or not. One of the most useful things about doing an internship is getting the exposure to and opportunity to practise workplace skills. From professionalism and working with others, to appropriately pitching your communications, you want to pick up as much as possible. The more you apply workplace skills the better an intern you will be, which is crucial to upping your chances of leaving with a good reference and potentially even a job offer.

Ending an internship: references and job offers

If your internship has gone well, the chances are that finishing it won't be the end of your relationship with the workplace. Firstly, you'll very likely want to call on them to provide you with a reference at some point. Secondly, there may be a job opportunity after it.

A workplace reference is a hugely valuable addition to an academic reference (see Chapter 14 on choosing your referees). Employers can get a good steer on your abilities and transferable skills from your academic reference; a workplace reference can additionally serve as an insight into what sort of employee you will be. Ensuring that you have performed well in your internship and that you have built good relationships with your mentor/line manager and colleagues are essential to getting a good reference. As with all references, seek permission appropriately. When you leave, ask your mentor/line manager whether they would be prepared to be a referee in the future.

Potential job opportunities arising out of an internship will be affected by your study and work plans. It's becoming more common, for example, for second year undergraduate students to do an internship during the summer before their third year. For those interning at the end of their studies, some will have plans set up for after their internship, perhaps a further degree course or a job. If you are available to take up a job offer after an internship, make that clear from the very start – in your interview. Many employers see internships as a way to try out prospective employees, so make sure that they know you're in the market. Having said that, job offers aren't limited to immediately after your internship. Employers might wait until you have finished your studies, or for a role to become vacant, and may well get in touch in the future. Don't feel you have to wait for the organization to get hold of you, however. It's always worth getting in touch when you're available to see if there are any openings.

Making a good last impression

Just as with leaving a work experience placement, make sure you thank everyone who's helped you. As well as being polite, making a good *last* impression is as important as making a good first impression – for the reasons we've been discussing: a good reference and leaving as a good prospective hire. As well as thanking your mentor/line manager, it's also worth asking for feedback on what you could usefully now develop. This might inform your next work experience move, as well as any decision-making on further study.

Maximizing the experience

Always ensure you make the most of any form of work experience you've gained in your job applications. Update your CV with each work experience placement, and if you worked on a specific project during an internship, make that clear in a short summary. When you are writing covering letters for job applications, remember to link your work experience to the skills and experience required in the role. Make sure you don't sell yourself short on your work experience, either. Something to keep in mind is that, particularly with technology-enabled remote working, doing work experience doesn't necessarily mean going into a workplace. If, for example, you have written a blog for a local newspaper, put that down as work experience. The same applies to volunteering. As we discussed in Chapter 1, both the transferable skills you develop and the specific tasks you undertake as a volunteer, can bolster your applications.

What I found useful:

'I made sure to apply for every internship or work experience opportunity my university offered. This meant that by the time I finished I had quite a lot of varied experience under my belt. Aside from looking good on my CV, it helped me feel more confident that I could be competent outside an academic setting and crack this whole real-world thing!'

What I wish I'd known:

'I wish I had realized that the vast majority of "successful" people try a lot of things after finishing university before they settle on the area in which they want to build a career. Before starting my Master's at Harvard University, I expected that my peers would have spent their twenties being focused and successful in one field. Instead, almost everyone had had a very busy twenties – but they each had tried a lot of very different paths, some of which had gone well and others not. Importantly, they were all still experimenting. If I had known that this experimenting phase lasted so long, I wouldn't have been so worried about making sure to do the "right" thing and instead just enjoyed being busy doing what I was doing at that moment in time.'

P.M. (PhD candidate)

Exercise

Where would your dream work experience take place? If you could do it anywhere at all, and it wasn't about what would be most 'useful'? Is it related to the area of work you are interested in or is it wildly different eg you've just finished a law degree and your dream work experience would be in conservation? It's worth spending a bit of time thinking about this. Firstly, it can be very helpful in focusing your mind on exactly what you're interested in, helping you to tailor your work experience as effectively as possible. It can also be helpful to give you some food for thought on what you might complement your working life with on a volunteering basis. Work won't be the only outlet for your interests, passions and talents, and employers are becoming increasingly keen on giving employees time to do some voluntary work during working hours.

04
Further study

When considering further study, you need to ask yourself some key questions. First and foremost, *why* are you thinking about continuing your studies? You want to avoid at all costs a situation where you're considering further study because you're not sure what else to do. In this chapter we'll look at exactly where further study fits into your priorities and where it would potentially fit into your career plans.

Main types of further study

Before we work through different motivations for taking up further study, let's briefly run through an overview of the main further study routes.

It's useful to break postgraduate further study down into two broad strands: what we'll refer to as further 'academic' study (higher degrees, such as a Master's or a PhD) and further 'vocational' study, namely study directly connected to a specific career path, for example, law or teaching. Within academic further study, the purpose and format will vary, but a Master's degree will often be followed by employment outside academia, whereas a PhD is commonly, though by no means exclusively, a route into a career in academia. Within vocational further study, the most common variant is the conversion course. These are intensive courses that allow you to pursue a profession that your undergraduate degree didn't focus on. The one-year Graduate Diploma in Law (GDL) and the Postgraduate Certificate in Education (PGCE) are two of the most popular, but there are also examples in fields from psychology to engineering. Graduate entry courses are another variant of vocational further study. They include medicine and dentistry and are generally four or five years long.

Other forms of further study

Further study can also include professional training, where you study as part of your professional development for the job you are in. In such cases, the training may be a professional requirement and your employer may pay for it.

It's worth emphasizing that further study courses that traditionally lead to a particular profession don't automatically preclude alternative career paths. For example, a PhD might lead to a role outside academia, where an in-depth understanding of a subject area is applied in a non-academic context; and legal training might lead to a job within the field of law other than that of a lawyer. Transferable skills developed through a further degree might also be applied in a completely different context. For example, the research and analytical skills honed through a PhD may be applied in a business context with no connection to the subject area studied.

Key questions to think about

Your decision to do further study will centre on three main questions:

→ Should I carry on in education?

→ Where would I study?

→ How would I pay for it?

What stage are you currently at in your planning? Are you considering further study as one of several options, or are you pretty clear that it is something you plan to do?

Reasons to consider further study

Let's look at some of the most common reasons for pursuing further studies, to see where your thinking fits in. Common reasons for considering further study include:

- it's necessary for getting into a particular profession;
- to enhance your employability;
- to pursue your interest in a subject;
- to shift direction from your current focus/career path;
- to develop a specific set of skills;
- to improve your academic record;
- you don't know what to do next;
- you haven't succeeded in getting a job;
- you enjoy the student lifestyle.

Deciding whether to do further study

Let's now look at what to weigh up to decide whether further study is your best option. We'll start by splitting further studies into two categories, those that are essential for pursuing your preferred career path and those that are not essential. If the decision is basically made for you – further study is required to get into the profession you've chosen – your choices are more straightforward. You do, however, still have research to do: on the most suitable institution and type of course, and on how you will fund it (discussed on page 41). If further study is *not* essential for your career path, you need to consider your case for studying longer carefully.

Non-essential further study: will it enhance your employability?

Do you really need to study more? Although pursuing further studies can be very well regarded by employers, there have been complaints that an increase in people studying longer today has become a distraction. Some industry leaders, for example, have argued that too many young people today go on to do a Master's degree, when what they really need is experience in the workplace. As a music industry employer notes, 'Getting a Master's isn't going to help: we're looking for well-rounded people and the skills we need are often more likely to have been gained through experience.' In contrast with this view, however, other employers say that a higher degree is something that they see as an asset in a candidate. They argue that in an increasingly 'congested' job market, having higher qualifications than other candidates can give you a competitive edge. The most widely applicable view lies somewhere in between: the advantages of doing further study will be case specific.

Insider insights: researching common career paths

To ascertain what will best serve your chances of getting a job, start by looking at career paths into the area of work you're interested in. Are there various ways in? Is there a path most commonly taken? Research and talk to the experts on this: look up and speak to professionals in the field. One way to research career profiles is through the 'About us' and 'Who we are' pages on workplace websites. If you get the opportunity, it's also very valuable to ask people working in the industry you're interested in for their advice. Something especially useful about doing work experience is getting a better understanding of what will help you to get into a particular industry. Ask the person who is supervising you for their views on whether further study will enhance your career prospects within their sector.

Other useful sources of insider information are students currently completing the course you're thinking about. When you're researching institutions to study at, ask to speak to current students when you go to the open day (and *always* go to the open day): why did they choose to do the course, and are they optimistic about where it will take them? If you don't get the chance to speak to current students, institutions often have student profiles on their websites addressing these types of questions. Be aware, however, that you are likely to be getting the most positive views in these write-ups.

Timings

A key consideration when considering a further study course is timing: the length of the course and the stage at which you can do it. You might find that there are courses that take a year at one institution but two years at another, for example. With the longer course, consider what added value there is to justify extending your studies further, and as we'll discuss, your finances.

When can you take a course? Master of Business Administration (MBA) courses, for example, often require candidates to have a minimum of three years' relevant full-time post-graduation work experience. This requirement is based on the premise that what is covered on an MBA is enhanced by students being able to apply their own industry experience. With other types of courses that *can* be taken straight after finishing your undergraduate degree there is an argument for applying a related logic. Returning to further study having spent some time in employment can extend the value of your course – both by how much *you* value it, having had time out from study, and how you're able to apply it to the 'real world'. You may also find that the industry knowledge you gain through employment helps you to choose the course that will be most beneficial to your next career move.

Pursuing a passion and other reasons for further study

Listed earlier were also some of the reasons for thinking about further studies that are less career related, those linked instead to your interests. As you're reading a careers guide, you won't be surprised to hear that the priority here is to link further study with career building. Where the motivation for wanting to do further study is less directly 'utilitarian', it's worth bearing two considerations in mind. The first is whether there isn't a way to connect your interest in your studies to your career plan. The second is whether you can afford to prioritize interests at this stage, career-wise and financially. If you have the financial opportunity to pursue your studies purely out of passion, you may want to consider this as a gap year.

And finally, there are cases where the motivation for doing further study is, to put it plainly, misguided. Ranging from simply not knowing what to do next, to preferring later morning starts, being a student for the sake of it isn't really a good enough reason – and you'll find yourself seriously struggling to write a persuasive personal statement when it comes to applying for courses.

Making an informed decision about which course to do

If you've decided that doing further study *is* the right thing to do to progress your career, or it's necessary for your targeted profession, the next thing to research is where to do it. As with your undergraduate degree, you will be considering both institutions and courses when choosing where to apply. The reputation of the institution, in terms of excellence rankings and future success records for students, is one factor. The other important factors relate to the day-to-day running of the course. What are the facilities like? Is the course content specifically what you're after? Is the course recognized in the industry you're targeting? Does the design of the course chime with your preferred learning and assessment style? If you're hoping to improve your academic record, how you think you will perform on the course is clearly particularly important.

Your ultimate aim should be to get into the most highly regarded institution that provides the type of course and learning experience you are looking for. It's easier to gauge an institution's reputation through league tables; harder is to garner evidence about the everyday realities of a course. As we mentioned earlier, a good way to get some insight into what a course has to offer is to speak to as many 'insiders' as possible: students taking the course and course tutors and lecturers. On the subject of inside knowledge, you may be wondering whether you should carry on your studies at the same institution as your undergraduate degree. Apply exactly the same questions and scrutiny as you would to any other institution, from reputation to course design.

Applying for further study

In many respects the application process for further study courses will be the bit that feels most familiar. Although postgraduate course applications can differ significantly from undergraduate applications, there is often considerable crossover. Your primary aim will be to demonstrate through your application – chiefly via a personal statement – that you will excel on the course. Course directors will want to know why you want to take the course and how it fits into a career plan, and be provided with evidence that you will do well in it. Having thought through the questions we've been looking at in this chapter – from your motivation for doing further study to why you have chosen a particular institution – you will be well placed to write a persuasive personal statement.

It goes without saying that the starting point for your application should be to ensure that you fulfil the basic eligibility requirements. Many – although not all – Master's courses require a minimum 2:1 degree classification, for example. Some conversion and graduate entry courses require you to have done particular subjects at GCSE or A level, or have completed a degree in a specific field.

A final consideration when you're applying for further study is who you approach to be your referees. Choose referees who will be able to bolster your application with insights into your relevant academic and work experience.

As ever, when your referees have confirmed that they are happy to provide you with a reference, brief them well. Provide an outline of why you want to do the course and how it fits into your career plans, as well as your relevant academic strengths, study to date and work experience. (For more on how to secure strong references, see Chapter 14.)

Paying for further study

Thinking about how you will pay for your course should ideally be part of your very early thinking on whether or not to pursue further studies. So, what are your options? Broadly speaking, there are two: having your study paid for through external funding, and paying for study through savings, loans or financial help from relatives.

In the case of external funding, there are two main types of sources: funding in the form of 'studentships', 'fellowships' or grants (for example, awarded through Research Councils UK, or 'learned' societies, such as the British Academy, and charitable trusts, such as the Wellcome Trust), and bursaries (available, for example, for some teacher training, social work and healthcare courses). It's also worth noting that sometimes employers offer sponsorship; however, this tends to be funding for continuing professional development (CPD), rather than postgraduate courses. These qualifications are usually awarded by the professional body within the relevant industry.

When you're researching funding opportunities, a first port of call should be your university or college's careers service. They will have detailed information on what funding is available nationally for the course you are looking at, as well as information about other funding opportunities, such as grants on offer for students or alumni of your current institution.

The careers service is also the place to get digestible details about the loans available to you. The government offers postgraduate study loans for many courses, such as a Postgraduate Master's Loan and a Postgraduate Doctoral Loan. Government loans may be your best borrowing option, in terms of interest rates and repayment conditions, but you still need to scrutinize the T&Cs. It's vital that you are clear on the future implications of taking out a postgraduate loan, and remember that you will need to cover both course fees and living costs. A good idea is to work out exactly what your expenditure for the duration of your course will be so that you can see what sort of financial commitment you are considering. You are looking at taking on potentially significant debt, so weighing up the future value of this investment is essential. It's also worth emphasizing that you will likely *already* have taken out a student loan for your undergraduate studies. As such, bear in mind that you will be looking at further increasing the amount of debt you take on.

In many cases, further study ends up being paid for through a combination of sources. Something to consider when you are working out how to pay for your studies is part-time work, such as an evening or weekend job. Don't bank on it in your budgeting, however, until you are sure about its feasibility. Many conversion courses, for example, are simply too intensive to allow time for paid work on the side. You might also find that when it comes to trying to get a part-time job, you can't find work that suits your course hours. Again, it's useful to talk to tutors and students from the course you want to do to see what they advise.

The other way to think about combining study and work is by doing further studies part-time or even via distance learning while you're working full-time. These are options more suited to a point where you are already established in a job, but they're a reminder that it's not now or never for further study.

Whatever you do, you can keep learning

Further study doesn't need to be an alternative to getting a job. And you certainly don't need to stop learning just because you've stopped your full-time education. As well as part-time study and professional development courses, there are many ways to learn new skills that can fit in with full-time work. Evening classes, online courses and weekend workshops provide an array of opportunities for you to use your spare time to enhance your CV and employability.

What I found useful:

'The cost of many Master's programmes exceeds the maximum Student Finance England loan available. Knowing that the programme I wanted to do cost several thousand pounds more than the available loan, I began looking around for additional sources of funding early on. By starting early, I was able to put together a strong application for a bursary from the university I was applying to. Institutional bursaries can sometimes be more likely to yield results than applying for funding elsewhere, so devoting time to seeing what your university is able to offer you is really worthwhile.'

What I wish I'd known:

'Doing a one-year Master's course I've found that there isn't the same time to "settle in" or adjust to new surroundings as there is during undergraduate studies. With hindsight, I would now recommend using the week or so before the programme starts to draw up a list of things you want to achieve, the lecturers who will be especially useful to liaise with and the kinds of societies that may bring you into contact with people who can assist you career-wise, etc.'

A.J. (Master's student)

Exercise

Whether you're aiming to undertake further study or not, what additional forms of learning might be helpful to your career development? Can you identify an evening or online course that would be beneficial to the skills you need to develop?

Part Two
Developing job-ready skills

05
Leadership and teamwork

Developing your leadership and teamwork might sound like you need to work on a set of new, specialist skills. But in practice, both leadership and teamwork boil down to how you interact with other people, and you'll almost certainly already have some relevant experience under your belt. We'll discuss their differences, but in many respects being a good leader and being a good team worker are highly interchangeable. Both skill sets are about working well with and getting the best out of other people – and yourself.

In the job application process, employers try to elicit candidates' leadership and teamwork skills in different ways. Sometimes assessment centre tests are used to observe how a potential employee interacts with colleagues. Alternatively, employers may ask you directly about your leadership and teamwork skills, usually asking for examples of when you've put them to use. So, as well as getting you to think about your own experiences and which ones to highlight, the purpose of this chapter is to become really familiar with what employers are getting at when they talk about good leaders and good team players.

Leadership

You don't need to be applying for a job where you'd be managing staff for employers to want to gauge your leadership skills. Equally, you don't have to be a boss to prove your leadership qualities in a job. And you don't even need to have had a job to demonstrate your leadership skills – you can draw on relevant experience from all areas of your life.

Your leadership record

Let's start by looking at your leadership record. Have you ever been a leader? You almost certainly have. Have you, for example, ever organized a team or event at university or college? Have you led a class group project, a school council meeting, a sports team or perhaps an extracurricular activity, such as a trip or a club? Or have you ever had to take charge in a paid work context, for example leading shifts in a part-time job? Have you ever set up and run your own 'venture' for example, regular babysitting? Or has voluntary work ever given you a chance to burnish your leadership skills, perhaps running a stall at a bring-and-buy sale, or organizing participants for a local event?

Thinking back to all these types of scenarios, you'll likely find that there have been multiple occasions where you've exercised leadership. Now the question is: how *well* did you lead?

Good leadership

Let's break good leadership down into key features. Some of these features focus more on the approach of the leader, and others more on how you treat those you're leading. You'll notice that the characteristics often interlink. You'll also notice that some add up to an overarching characteristic – for example 'fairness' and 'honesty' might be described together as 'integrity'.

> **TIP:** *Ask as many people as possible if they can think of a good boss they've had – if they can, what are three things that made that boss effective?*

So, what does good leadership in the workplace look like?

- **Taking responsibility.** The extent to which the buck starts and stops with you will vary, but a hallmark of good leadership is being prepared to take responsibility. This may come in the form of taking the initiative to get something started, sorting out a problem, or taking the blame for a decision that has gone wrong.

- **Being decisive.** Being able to make decisions and stick to them is vital. You can't solve a problem if you can't be decisive about a course of action, and you can't initiate a project if you can't settle on how to do it.

- **Being innovative.** Innovation in this context is partly about creative and critical thinking, and partly about responding to new information in a dynamic way – or, put more simply, changing your mind when necessary. Note that being decisive doesn't mean being immovable on decisions.

- **Being fair.** Fairness plays a really important role in getting the best out of people, because it means that they know rewards come down to hard work and talent rather than arbitrary whim or favour.

- **Being clear.** Clarity about your expectations and the relevant practicalities of the task or project are essential to enabling your colleagues to be productive. You need to be very clear about the goal you're seeking to achieve, what the process to achieve it will look like, and each person's specific role.

- **Having expertise.** Having expertise is an important justification for being in a leadership role. This isn't about being expert at everything. It is about having a level of relevant experience and knowledge that means you can lead with authority, teach other people and identify what is required to complete pieces of work.

- **Being confident.** Taking charge requires the confidence that you can lead well. If you don't believe in yourself, neither will those you're leading. The authority achieved through expertise and knowing what you're doing helps pave the way for confidence.

- **Delegating.** You won't have the time or skills to do everything yourself, and you are wasting a team you don't use. Giving others suitable responsibilities and tasks is a core leadership skill. It involves being able to identify who can best take on a job and coordinating well by articulating clear expectations.

- **Trusting people.** While you will sometimes need to be critical about colleagues' work, to get the best out of them, alongside this you need to be able to trust them to do their job. A key part of delegating, for example, is trusting that your colleagues will do their assigned tasks properly. A key part of developing staff is about giving them the opportunity to prove that they can be trusted.

- **Motivating others.** Inspiring others is a vital ingredient of good leadership. This is as much about how you present the tasks to be done as it is about how you encourage people to do their best work.

- **Having drive.** If you're going to lead a successful team, the desire to succeed is imperative. Achieving successful outcomes is a strong indication of good leadership, so you need the drive to motivate not just yourself but also your colleagues to fulfil your aims.

- **Being supportive.** Your colleagues will need your support to develop and when things go wrong. You want loyal staff who support your aims with their efforts and commitment, so give and take is required on both sides.

- **Developing others**. A good leader is always on the lookout for ways to promote their colleagues' professional development and experience. This isn't just about being a supportive boss who is interested in their career progress, it's about getting the most out of people.

- **Feeding back**. An essential element of developing your staff is giving them feedback. Highlighting when staff are performing well, with positive feedback, is as important as constructive criticism on how to improve.

- **Showing appreciation**. Recognizing people's efforts is essential to motivating them. You work harder when you feel your hard work is valued.

- **Going that bit further**. Part of being a good leader is being prepared to go that bit further and having the work ethic to realize this. This isn't about staying the longest in the office or getting more stressed than everyone else; it's about always striving to reach the highest standards.

- **Being honest**. Being honest is essential for people to know where they stand. If a project is going to be difficult, employees need to be aware from the start to ensure they plan in the necessary time and resources. If work has been poorly done, an employee needs to know in order to remedy it. If you, as a leader, screw up, you need to acknowledge it so your colleagues see that you hold yourself to the same standards.

- **Being approachable and building relationships**. Working with people is all about building relationships, and people respond better when they're led by someone they can relate to. While you want to maintain boundaries, do take an interest in your colleagues' lives outside work, and don't be afraid to make conversation about things other than work. Being approachable is also about being able to empathize with your staff. If an employee has a personal problem that might affect their work, you want them to feel able to come and discuss this with you.

- **Respecting boundaries**. Although we do want 'humans' to lead us, good leaders know where to draw the line. This is about being professional and knowing what to leave outside the workplace. Bad day? *Never* take it out on your colleagues.

Practising your leadership

Each aspect of good leadership outlined above can be applied to your work at any stage of your career development. Whether it's showing appreciation, taking initiative, being fair or going that bit further, implement these approaches to how you operate today, and they'll serve you well both now and in the future. This is why good leadership skills are often described by employers simply as 'the skills you need to succeed in life' – and why employers are so keen to see these in the people they hire.

Testing scenarios

It's much easier to be a good leader when things are going your way. Difficult situations are the best test of leadership. So, let's look at how you might handle a tricky workplace situation, using a hypothetical scenario.

Scenario:

A colleague you line manage is scheduled to do a presentation to clients. Ten minutes before he is due to start, he realizes that he has deleted the folder containing the presentation slides and accompanying notes.

What to do?

First identify the problem so that you can solve it. There is no presentation for the clients who are about to arrive. Your solution needs to be swiftly determined as there is very little time. Together with your colleague you will present without notes or slides. Your understanding of the presentation brief is enough to be able to step in, and your trust in your colleague means that you have faith that he is well enough prepared to talk through the presentation. You will support your colleague by co-presenting, and you will be honest with the client by letting them know that there has been a technical problem.

This is one set of responses to the scenario – there isn't of course a 'correct' answer, but you'll note that several of the good leadership skills discussed are applied. What else might you add or do differently?

Teamwork

What are teamwork skills? In short, the skills needed to work well in a group situation and good interpersonal skills. Working in a team might refer to working on a particular project with others, and it might refer to working in a team of colleagues on a day-to-day basis.

There is a good deal of overlap between good leadership and good teamwork, so rather than delineating the two, think of this section of the chapter as building on the leadership discussion. Both leading well and working effectively in a team centre on engaging with other people's contributions, and many of the characteristics of good leadership are the characteristics of a good team player. This isn't surprising: as a leader, you are also part of a team.

Teamwork experience

Think back to when you last worked in a team, at school, university/college, in paid work or in a leisure or voluntary role capacity. Although you may not consider teamwork to be a big component of your CV, you are likely to have spent a good deal of time working in a team of some form. Each time you worked with other people on a piece of work or project, or even played a game, you were practising 'teamwork skills'. Were you a good team worker? Can you identify what might have made you an asset to a team – or a burden? Being part of a team is not obviously the same as working well in a team. You might be contributing too little or thwarting progress by not cooperating well.

So, what do good teamwork skills in the workplace look like?

- **Joining in and pulling your weight.** Don't hang back and let the others do all the work – or be afraid to make your mark.

- **Taking an interest in others and their contributions.** If you're not interested in what the rest of your team is doing, you aren't doing a good job. You need to know what they're contributing to understand where and how your work fits in.

- **Delivering what you've agreed to, within the agreed timeframe.** Your colleagues are relying on you, and failing to meet a deadline means holding up the whole team's progress. Only agree to what you can achieve. If the proposed deadline is impossible to meet, make that clear from the start.

- **Sharing credit for your successes and recognizing the successes of others.** If you are working well within your team, your success is not going to be only down to you. As part of a team your success is also reliant on how well others do, and recognizing their achievements is vital for team morale.

- **Taking and giving feedback constructively, including criticism.** Part of the strength of working in a team is the opportunity to get feedback from colleagues. Take note and respond to feedback to strengthen and improve your work. When giving feedback, be clear, concise and diplomatic.

- **Valuing different types of team players and contributions.** Team members will differ hugely, both in how they communicate and in what they bring to the table. Don't fall into the trap of valuing the more vocal over the more thoughtful. Help make the team work by helping to draw in team members who are quieter.

- **Taking responsibility for the overall goal not just your role or task in it.** Don't be tempted to just 'do your job'. Part of your job is fitting your contribution into the wider work of the team.

- **Making clear contributions.** Make sure you are clear in your own mind about what you want to say and do, and that it has value, before putting it forward. There is nothing like lack of clarity to undermine how persuasive you are.

- **Being open-minded and not taking sides.** Being closed-minded risks shutting yourself off from good ideas and new ways of approaching a problem. Your interest should be in working towards solutions rather than simply taking sides in a discussion or disagreement.

- **Disagreeing well.** Difference of opinion in teams is not only inevitable but one of the benefits of getting several heads together. Constructive debate about how to do something and navigating conflicting views are often the way that brilliant ideas are developed. Be tactful in both how you express your disagreement and how you respond to your own views being rejected.

What *not* to do in a team meeting

Don't:

- monopolize discussion;
- contribute for the sake of it;
- come unprepared;
- switch off when others talk.

Your teamwork record

Think back to a recent scenario when you were working in a team. How many of the teamwork skills above did you exercise? Where could you improve? Now think of a scenario where you were on a team with a frustrating team member. What made their contribution problematic?

As well as thinking about your teamwork record in terms of your skills, you want to be able to identify examples of your teamwork experience to showcase to prospective employers. It's helpful to have one or two stand-out examples up your sleeve. The situation itself can vary, but you want to make sure there is scope to clearly illustrate how your skills contributed to the team's success. Take membership of a debating club, for example. You might pick a debating event where the team won as an indicator of success, and you could then point to a range of teamwork skills examples, from working together to form the argument to organizing travel arrangements.

The foundation for a good team

Respecting other people's work, time, views and approaches is an important foundation for effective teams. But good teamwork isn't only about good team members; being able to perform well in a team also relies on having the right circumstances:

- a common goal;
- a clear task and timetable;
- opportunity for everyone to contribute;
- well-organized coordination.

Lack of clarity in particular – unclear tasks, timing or purpose – can be the undoing of a team's effectiveness. In short, and joining up the dots between leadership and teamwork, a well-run team needs to be well led.

TIP: *If you have a contribution to make in a meeting, jot it down. We're often so busy rehearsing what we want to say that we stop listening to the discussion. By writing your point down, you won't need to think about it again until you say it.*

What I found useful:

'Having a research career, I frequently work alone but still need the typical leadership and interpersonal skills of any workplace. What I found particularly useful to this end was committing time to an extra curricula CV. For me it was the Army Reserve, but it could be anything – sport, charity work, events organizing, etc – that goes beyond the comfort zone and pushes you to embrace new skills, walks of life and experiences, all of which feeds directly back into the day job.'

What I wish I'd known:

'When I was younger, I never thought of myself as a leader per se – or aspired to be one. Something I wish I'd known then was that leadership is not always the same as being in charge, and good teamwork tends to require leadership skills from all its members at one time or another. In my experience, whatever the role or size of group, these include the drive to shape more than be shaped by a problem and an emphasis on getting the best out of those around you.'

J.R. (Pollster)

Exercise

Going through the list of good leadership skills, which do you think you would score well on and which do you think you need to develop? Now go back to your own leadership practice examples. Do you think any improvements in your leadership skills would have altered outcomes? Repeat the same process for teamwork skills. How do you fare?

06
Communication skills

When you think about communication skills in a workplace context, public speaking or deploying the powers of persuasion in business pitches may come to mind. But as with so many aspects of working life, communication skills also refer to skills you'll be well practised in. From how you communicate in conversation and how you write, to the non-verbal signals you give off through your body language, we're talking about skills that you've been using throughout your life. When employers talk about good communication skills, they're ultimately looking for the skills that enable you to express yourself articulately and to work well with other people.

Specifically, good workplace communication skills include:

- producing writing that is clear and to the point;
- having a good phone manner;
- sending clearly written emails, professional in tone and typo free;
- getting on and working well with your colleagues;
- conveying your ideas and opinions persuasively;
- giving presentations and speeches that are clear and compelling;
- gathering information effectively;
- giving feedback;
- being a helpful contributor in meetings.

Communicating effectively won't only help you to succeed in the workplace, it will help you to *get* there. Throughout the job application process, employers will be looking at the way you express yourself. From how clearly and persuasively you write your covering letter, to how articulately you describe relevant experience in an interview, your communication skills will be an important factor in prospective employers' decision-making. In this chapter we'll go through examples of how to communicate well in a variety of workplace scenarios. These will help you to understand what employers are after and highlight which skills you can put into practice now.

Soft communication skills

Most of what you do at work involves some form of communication. There's the content of your output and there are your general interactions, verbal and non-verbal, with other people. Honing your communication skills, therefore, isn't limited to working on what you might call 'formal' activities such as report writing and public speaking. A good chunk of life at work involves social interaction eg social niceties, sharing space, impromptu chat, etc. These interactions are crucial to working relationships and bring in what can be described as the 'soft' communication skills that convey how you treat other people.

Your behaviour towards others, and even your physical demeanour, contribute to how you communicate in the workplace. Non-verbal communication such as body language can draw people to you if it's friendly and open, or alienate them if it's aggressive or defensive or withdrawn. Equally, verbal courtesy, such as greeting people when you enter a room, signals your awareness of, and respect for, others.

Here are some key ways to communicate positively towards others in the workplace:

1 Keep your body language open and your tone and expression friendly.

2 Respect other people's physical space and property.

3 Maintain good eye contact in conversation.

4 Be considerate eg don't leave an empty milk carton in the fridge when you've finished it, do keep private phone calls short and quiet.

5 Avoid distracting people, for example with loud or long non-work-related conversations.

6 Be empathetic: consider other people's feelings and take an interest in people's wellbeing.

7 Practise courtesy eg offer to make a drink for others when you make your own.

8 Mind your manners: greet and thank when appropriate.

You'll notice that the examples given here are ones that could apply in any context. What are essentially basic principles of behaving well go a long way in brokering good relationships in the workplace.

Communicating in meetings

A meeting at work could be a quick catch-up with a colleague or a half-day brainstorming session with your whole office and a team of clients. While the format and purpose of meetings will vary, the skills you'll be deploying will have the same aim. Thinking back to the last chapter on teamwork, key to working well in a team is getting the best out of it with effective interpersonal skills. This applies to meetings, where you are also working collaboratively, be it with your team, with clients or both, so let's recap on the relevant basics:

- Contribute to the discussion and make your contributions clear and relevant.
- Engage with what others are saying.
- Be clear on what you and others are agreeing to deliver or follow up on.
- Take and give feedback on viewpoints and contributions constructively.
- Be open-minded and don't take sides.
- Disagree well.

Good question

Something else to bring into meetings are those skills that help you to gather information. How you ask questions and how you clarify points that have been made can determine whether you go away with a full understanding or not.

The way a question is phrased can impact on the answer, so make your questions short, clear and neutral. Don't lead up to your question with a long preamble: get straight to what you want to ask and ask it in a way that isn't leading. For example, rather than asking: 'When you say the product will be ready soon, am I correct in assuming you mean next week?' Instead ask, 'When will the product arrive?' Part of good questioning is listening. It goes without saying that your question is redundant if it was already answered when you weren't paying attention. Employers often ask candidates if they have any questions at the end of an interview. As a senior executive at an advertising agency put it, don't turn your questions into an own goal: 'Too often I'll get questions at the end of the interview that I've already answered – showing me that (a) the candidate wasn't listening to what I was saying and (b) that they turned up with a pre-prepared question rather than asking a "real" question.'

Communicating from afar

These days our work is increasingly done over the phone, via platforms such as Skype, and via email and instant messaging. So how we communicate remotely matters more than ever.

While email has overtaken phone calls as the way to communicate from afar, there will always be occasions where a work call is necessary. Whether it's a brief catch-up call on the phone, or a Skype tele-conference, the basic good communication rules apply. Keep what you have to say on the phone clear, concise and purposeful; listen carefully and clarify where necessary; and implement 'soft' communication skills, for example, by wishing the other person a nice evening at the end of the call. Have a standard response for answering external calls, including an appropriate greeting, the name of your workplace and your name. In an open-plan office consider your colleagues when on the phone: avoid talking and laughing very loudly.

Email

There will be cases where your only communication with a work contact is email, so emailing professionally is essential. Employers will get some insight into your emailing skills through emailed applications – where errors such as a misspelt name or the wrong title *are* noticed – and sometimes inbox exercises will be used as assessments in the application process.

Here are some basic email guidelines to follow:

- **Subject line.** Always use the subject line and use it accurately – if you are emailing for advice, for instance, do not put 'Hello' as the subject.
- **Addressing your recipient.** Make sure you get names and titles right and use the appropriate level of formality in your greeting. Keep in mind that 'appropriate' applies to *in*formality as much as it does to formality; for example, if the recipient comes back with a 'Hi' rather than a 'Dear', respond accordingly.

- **Punctuation.** Always use correct capitalization and punctuation – it simply makes your emails easier to read.

- **Proofreading.** Read your emails back for typos as well as to see if they make sense, and set your email account to automatically spellcheck every email you send.

- **Sign-off.** Pick and stick to an appropriate and professional sign-off, such as 'Best wishes' or 'Kind regards'.

- **Signature.** Make sure all your details are correct (you'd be amazed by how often people spell their street wrong or miss out a phone number digit).

It's also worth following these basic guidelines to avoid some common email pitfalls:

- **Get the tone right.** As a rule, keep your tone friendly and professional but do also respond to specific circumstances appropriately. If, for example, you are replying to an email that notified you about bad personal news, do express sympathy and consider adjusting your sign-off accordingly. Be cautious about using humour in an email unless you know the recipient well, as it can easily be misread as sarcasm or rudeness.

- **Ensure you're emailing who you're intending to.** Always double check that the email's recipients are who you mean to email – with autofill it can be easy to send a message to the wrong person. If you do send an email in error, alert the unintended recipient immediately.

- **Avoid 'Reply All'.** There are relatively few occasions when replying to everyone in a large group email is necessary, so do so with caution. Be particularly wary of carrying out a lengthy discussion in which not everyone receiving the email is involved. Misusing 'Reply All' just clogs up people's inboxes and can be irritating.

- **Never email in anger.** *Always* avoid emailing in a moment of anger or frustration. If you find yourself in such a situation, wait a few hours before responding. After you've cooled off you can write an email making your feelings clear but in a way that is level-headed and civil. Angry emails are not only unprofessional, they can come back to bite you, either because you regret sending them or because they get circulated to others.

- **Forward with care.** Before forwarding an email, double check there isn't content earlier in the thread that isn't meant for a wider audience. Whether it's a confidential discussion or your detailed Friday night plans, be sure that you and your fellow correspondent(s) would be happy to share it.

- **Avoid 'sensitive' content.** Think twice before sending any sensitive emails from your work account – be they gossipy or off colour. A useful test is whether you'd be embarrassed if an email was seen by your boss: if so, don't send it.

- **Use emoticons sparingly.** When used appropriately, a smiley face can convey what a thousand words can't – but they can also be seen as over-familiar and unprofessional, so keep them for close colleagues, and avoid overusing them.

- **Steer clear of slang and 'text-speak'.** Keep your email style professional, avoiding overly casual language and abbreviations.

TIP: Don't sit on emails for days without replying: if you know it will take some time to come back with an answer on something, send a holding note acknowledging the email and giving an approximate timeframe for when you will get back in touch.

Email, phone or face-to-face?

Part of communicating well in a workplace is picking the most appropriate communication method. A good general principle is to communicate face-to-face for complicated or sensitive scenarios and situations where something needs to be extensively discussed; to use email for straightforward correspondence or when you need a written record to refer back to; and to use the telephone (or equivalent) for scenarios that sit somewhere in between.

Choosing the best communication method

Would you arrange a meeting, pick up the phone or send an email in the scenarios below? What are your reasons?

- You want to talk to your boss about a pay rise because you feel that your workload has increased.

- You need to confirm the timings of a conference with an external contact.

- You want greater clarity about the price of a job that is being done for you by an outside agency.

General writing

Whatever type of job you have, at some point you will have to do some writing. Whether it's an article, a project update or a set of instructions, your aim should be the same: to express yourself clearly and concisely. You also want to fulfil the core purpose of your writing, be it to inform or to persuade.

The two main components of good writing are the clarity of *what* you are trying to articulate (your thinking and purpose) and the clarity of *how* you articulate this (how you construct your writing).

Here are some general writing guidelines that will help you achieve clarity and conciseness:

Content rules to apply to your writing

- Be clear about what you want to say before you start. What are you aiming to do through this piece of writing?

- Write out a structure using section headings. Think out each section you need and then organize these into the most logical order. What should you start with to capture attention and end with to conclude most effectively?

- Write out a draft. Use your section headings, opening and end to build up your first draft.

- Edit. Go through your draft, clarifying your thoughts by removing repetition or unnecessary details and elaborating further where necessary.

Structure and style rules to apply to your writing

- Shorten very long sentences.

- Avoid using jargon and keep your language simple.

- Write in the style appropriate for the audience, for example with regards to the level of formality.

- Break up your writing into paragraphs and well signposted sections.

- Use punctuation and grammar properly and proofread your writing at least twice.

- Present your writing neatly, legibly (check font size), and with a clear start and finish.

Public speaking

There's a perception that public speaking is a talent, rather than a skill, and that some people are naturally good at it and others not. While some people may be less daunted by the prospect of public speaking, anyone can learn to speak well in public if they are armed with the right tools and strategies.

The key to effective public speaking is good preparation: for what you are going to say and for how you are going to deliver it. Both strong content and strong delivery are required for a good speech. An incoherent set of thoughts delivered with panache will fail, as will a well-structured speech delivered inaudibly.

Preparing what you're aiming to achieve

Your goal when speaking in public is to get people to listen to you – and to keep their attention. When you have a public speaking task ahead of you, the first thing to do is nail down your aim. What are you trying to do with your speech? Are you primarily trying to inform or educate, or are you trying to persuade? If your aim is to inform or educate, your main task is to impart information so that it is remembered. This comes down to presenting it clearly and succinctly and in a way that is interesting and engaging. A good way to help engage an audience is with powerful stories and human examples.

If your job is to persuade, for example to convince people to subscribe to a particular viewpoint, the power of your speech lies in the strength of your argument. Is your argument logical? Does it withstand critical questioning? Does it trump counter arguments? Whatever the purpose of your speech, passion and enthusiasm always help to sell something, be it a product or an argument, as does well-placed humour.

Let's now break public speaking down into a set of steps you can implement (also see Chapter 18 for further tips on delivering to an audience). You'll notice that one of the suggested steps below is to write your speech out in full; this is to work out exactly what you want to say – as well as to work out how much you can say in your given time slot. When it comes to the delivery of the speech, however, it can be more effective to use a set of bullet points to work from. Using a full prose 'script' from which to deliver a speech can lead to reading it word for word, removing dynamism from your delivery.

Step 1 – Constructing your speech

- Work out how many words you have time for, calculating that you speak at a rate of around 130–150 words per minute.

- Organize what you want to say into three parts.

- Write your speech out in clear language, avoiding jargon.

- Incorporate your most powerful point into your opening line.

- Outline what you are going to cover in your speech at the start.

- Summarize your main points in your conclusion.

- Consider whether you want to include some questions for the audience during your speech. If you do, work out when would be most effective, and how much time these will likely take up.

Step 2 – Preparing your materials

- Prepare two versions of your speech: one full version and one made up of just the main bullet points of what you will say. The bullet points should capture the essence of what you will be delivering, written with key words rather than full sentences. Use the bullet point version as your main tool for delivery, with the full version available for back up should you need it eg if your mind goes blank on some details. Insert each of your bullet points next to the relevant part of the text in the full version. This will help you to find where you are in your written out speech, should you need to work from it at any point.

- Print your full speech and bullet points in a large font, and make sure that each page is numbered.

- Practise with a timer and trim your speech if necessary. If you have decided to engage your audience with some questions, make sure you have factored in time to listen to, and where applicable, respond to, the answers.

- If you have time and a willing friend/colleague or relative, also practise in front of someone. It's a good chance to rehearse things like looking up while you're delivering your speech, as well as to check that you're not going too fast or speaking too quietly.

Step 3 – Delivering your speech

- Set up your notes so that you can comfortably see them, and make sure you have sight of a clock or your watch.

- Check that you have a glass of water within reach.

- Regularly look up at your audience during your delivery.

- Remember not to go too fast – deliberately slow yourself down when you start – and don't be afraid to pause.

Miscommunications

As with any environment where humans interact, work life is full of scope for misunderstandings and unintentional offending. Being clear in what you say, clarifying effectively and deploying your 'soft' communication skills will help to avoid such situations. They will arise at some point, however, so know how to handle miscommunication. Whether you are the source or subject of a miscommunication, keep the following principles in mind:

- Act swiftly, don't let the situation fester.

- Apologise unambiguously and sincerely.

- Give people the benefit of the doubt.

- Don't hold a grudge: accept an apology.

- Learn from the incident.

Listening is a communication skill

It might sound counterintuitive, but listening is a core communication skill. Every aspect of communication we have discussed is enhanced through listening. Indeed, a great number of misunderstandings in the workplace come down to people not listening to each other. Implement active listening, where you are not only listening properly but also checking your understanding through questions and clarifications. The art of good listening can also be applied to non-verbal communication, through empathy. Being aware of how other people are feeling will allow you to respond to them more appropriately.

What I found useful:

'This is my first full-time job and I have found observing how colleagues communicate – for example, how they answer the phone – a good way to pick up tips.'

What I wish I'd known:

'We're so used to using screens to communicate that I hadn't realized I would be using the phone until my interview when I was asked about my phone manner, which I hadn't thought about or practised. I wish I'd practised talking on the phone a lot more, for example by making appointments for the GP and dentist, and sorting out my mobile contract, rather than asking my mum or brother to do it for me!'

S.M. (Education programme assistant director)

Exercise

Go back to the last email you wrote. Think about the guidelines discussed for workplace emails. How does your last email compare? If it was an email to a friend or family member, what aspects would you need to change if you were emailing someone in a work context?

07
Problem-solving

Employers want to hire 'problem-solvers' for a number of reasons. An effective problem-solver in the workplace is someone who can think laterally and analytically; who will look at a problem logically but also creatively; and who is able to research, evaluate and analyse information to come up with solutions that are well informed and practical. A problem-solver is also someone who won't give up on a task and who won't panic during the process because they are under pressure. In short, effective problem-solving requires a skill set and a mindset.

But before we go any further, what do we actually mean by 'problems'? Life in general, as well as in the workplace, presents a constant flow of problems to solve. Whether it's working out why your car won't start, how to install a piece of software on your laptop, or how to brighten up your bedroom, we spend a great deal of our time working out solutions to problems. In the workplace, as well as figuring out how to unjam the printer, you'll be trying to think of ways to improve sales, develop a new programme or cover for someone who is ill. Problems, and therefore problem-solving, are an everyday part of work.

The key skills involved in problem-solving

Let's run through the key skills used in problem-solving to give you an idea of the breadth we're looking at. It's worth emphasizing that part of effective problem-solving is working out *which* skills you need to use.

As with all skill sets, problem-solving skills interlink. For example, your creativity skills might fuel your scope to take the initiative to change something for the better; your research skills might enable you to successfully negotiate because you're forearmed with all the relevant pros and cons. It's also worth having in mind that effective problem-solving draws on your wider skill set. Solving problems well is often reliant on good communication and teamwork, for example.

Key skills used in problem-solving:

- evaluating information;
- decision-making;
- using initiative;
- innovation and creativity;
- negotiation;
- research skills.

Problem-solving examples in your own life

The earlier description of an analytical, logical, lateral thinking and creative candidate who successfully solves problems may sound like a utopian one, but is actually well within reach.

Let's think about your own problem-solving record. It's useful to do this both to illustrate the skills we're looking at and to show you that you're already using these. Thinking back to just the past month, you'll see that you regularly face a whole range of situations that require you to problem-solve. We'll split these scenarios into two strands to highlight how diverse problem-solving is. Let's look at study-related and practical 'life' problems that you've recently handled. Below are a few examples to help prompt you:

Study-related problem-solving examples:

- You are really struggling with one of your courses.
- You need to submit an outline for your dissertation but can't decide between two different topics.

Practical problem-solving examples:

- Your halls of residence neighbour keeps playing loud music at night when you are trying to sleep.
- You want to go on a skiing trip and need to find a way to pay for it.

You'll notice that these scenarios require different types of solutions. They are about working out how to fix something, solving a dilemma, improving something and making something positive happen. This variety is important because it highlights that problem-solving is about skills that enable you to be proactive and foster good ideas, as well as to troubleshoot.

Drawing on the examples above, can you think of your own similar scenarios? Picking one example from your studies and one relating to a life practicality, how did you go about solving them at the time? And if you didn't solve them, what prevented you from doing so?

The basic steps of problem-solving

We've touched on the key skills involved in problem-solving and the types of scenarios you might have experienced. Let's now look at what effective problem-solving entails in a bit more detail. Different scenarios will require different tactics – some will be more complex and draw in more skills and considerations than others – but it's useful to break down the process of problem-solving into six basic steps.

Problem-solving in six steps

Step 1: Identify and define a problem.

Step 2: Identify the cause(s) of the problem.

Step 3: Consider potential solutions.

Step 4: Decide on the best solution.

Step 5: Implement the solution.

Step 6: Evaluate the impact of the solution.

Let's apply these steps to solving one of the earlier example problems:

Solving the problem of your halls of residence neighbour waking you up with their loud music

Step 1: You can't sleep properly between 11 pm and 2 am.

Step 2: Loud music coming through the wall from your neighbour's room late at night is waking you up repeatedly.

Step 3: You could ask your neighbour to turn their music down; you could get some earplugs; you could sleep at a different time.

Step 4: Asking your neighbour to turn their music down is the best course of action because it could stop rather than mitigate the problem.

Step 5: You ask your neighbour to turn their music down.

Step 6: You go to bed and find out whether loud music is played between 11 pm and 2 am.

The steps emphasize that solving problems is a dynamic process. You might find you need to go back a step, revaluate the evidence you have or reconsider a decision. For example, you might have wrongly identified the cause of the problem. Let's say it turns out not to be your neighbour playing loud music but the bar opposite. You might have chosen the wrong solution – you went for the earplugs, which turned out to be uncomfortable and inadequate against the noise. Or your solution might fail – you asked your neighbour to turn the music down, and they refused to. The process of problem-solving not only requires a methodical approach, its effectiveness is dependent on the success of each step.

Problem-solving skills in practice

Let's now look at a breakdown of the skills you might apply to find effective solutions. In each case we'll also look at an example of the sort of question you might get asked by employers to demonstrate how you'd use this skill in your problem-solving.

Evaluating information: to identify a problem and to analyse evidence

Problems don't necessarily make themselves evident, and employers want employees who are able to recognize that there is one. Bearing in mind that the 'problem' needn't be something that has gone wrong but can also be something that could be improved, here the skill is in identifying beneficial change. To do this you need to be able to fully evaluate the information you have about the current situation using critical thinking. You'll go on to examine the details of the problem to define the cause(s) and weigh up the information you have about potential solutions. Throughout your evaluations, your analysis requires scrutiny of the evidence, paying attention to the details.

Question: What information would you need to analyse in order to decide whether a new product is a success?

> **TIP:** *Be specific. Evaluation is about attention to detail. For example, rather than saying you would find out whether the product was selling well, say that you would compare the sales figures for the last month with a top-selling product.*

Research skills

Effective evaluation relies on good research skills as well as analytical thinking. Whether it's working out what's wrong with something, or developing new ideas, research skills are needed to gather the evidence that problem-solving requires. The foundation of good research is a methodical and critical approach. Not all evidence is useful, and not all information is reliable. Effective research skills are about being able to identify reliable sources and correct and pertinent information to inform your decisions. To do so, you need a systematic and clear research process to be able to investigate facts and to find, and be able to understand, appropriate and accurate data sources.

Question: How did you go about researching the organization before the interview?

> **TIP:** *You want to demonstrate your ability to use multiple sources and to judge which ones are reliable. So, don't just refer to what you have read on their website. Bring in write-ups from well-established trade publications, for example.*

Using initiative

In a workplace context, showing initiative means having the proactive mentality to get things started along with the resourcefulness to realize them.

Using your initiative is a skill that you will use at various points in problem-solving. For example, you might use initiative to identify that something could be done better if changes were implemented. Or you might use your initiative to fix a problem at work rather than asking your superior to fix it. The thread running through the idea of using initiative is taking on a problem independently.

Question: Would you describe yourself as a self-starter?

> **TIP:** *Your aim here is to demonstrate that you don't rely on being told what to do to work well and that you are capable of working independently. A good way to illustrate this is with an example of when you have succeeded when left to your own devices.*

Decision-making

You can't solve a problem without making decisions. As we discussed, the very act of problem-solving may have come down to deciding that something is not being done well enough. Decisions are made all the way through the problem-solving process, from analysing the issue and deciding what is causing it, to deciding what you will research to find the best solutions, to weighing up the resultant pros and cons and arriving at the optimal solution. How you make decisions is central to their effectiveness. Good decisions are made by arriving at logical conclusions, drawing on your research and evaluation skills to weigh up pros and cons and seeking advice from others to inform your verdicts.

Question: Give an example of a decision you made that turned out to be a mistake.

> **TIP:** *The aim here is to demonstrate your understanding of how to make decisions effectively by identifying what you did wrong. For example, if inadequate research led you to the wrong conclusion, outline how you would research the issue properly with hindsight.*

Innovation and creativity

A key part of successfully solving problems is coming up with new ideas and novel approaches. This is about using imagination and striving to think outside the box to come up with inventive but workable solutions. Innovation also means taking an enterprising approach to your work that leads you to seek out and recognize new opportunities. Innovation isn't only about coming up with creative new ideas, it's also about applying creativity and fresh thinking to existing situations and issues.

Question: How would you raise the charity's donations?

> **TIP:** *Your goal is to introduce a new way of thinking, or a new idea, to solve the problem. For example, you might propose an innovative way of improving a fundraising strategy already being used by the charity; or you might propose creatively adapting a money-making venture normally used outside the charity sector.*

Negotiation

A solution to a problem will in many cases require you to work with others – and potentially to negotiate with them at different points in the process. Negotiation isn't solely about finding a solution that works for everybody. It might also be about getting people to agree to tackle a problem in the first place. Ultimately, the aim of negotiation is to bring about agreement in the problem-solving process, allowing you to proceed to a mutually beneficial end. Your powers of persuasion will need to come into play in how you present your argument in discussions, as will your understanding of everybody's needs and your ability to identify potential criticisms or problems that they might raise. Communication skills therefore play an important role in negotiation, ensuring active listening to concerns and different perspectives, and articulating and expressing your viewpoint.

Question: Give an example of when you had to compromise with others in order to agree on a solution.

> **TIP:** *You want to showcase your understanding of effective negotiation in describing how you compromised. So, for example, listening to concerns in discussions about possible solutions, you could agree to revaluate your proposed solution with them after a trial period.*

Challenging circumstances

As well as being keen to see understanding and evidence of problem-solving skills, employers want to know whether you are able to handle problems in challenging circumstances.

Problem-solving under pressure

Generally, there'll be some form of pressure in the picture when you're solving a problem. A problem often needs to be solved quickly, putting you under time pressure. Or pressure may come in the form of expectations, that the outcome is satisfactory for everyone involved, for example. Whatever the source of the pressure, being able to stay level-headed and focused is vital. Thinking back to team skills and leadership, how you deal with pressure also affects those you work with. Working relationships need to run particularly smoothly when the deadline is tight or the task very difficult. How you react to pressure can affect how you communicate. A sense of panic can lead to a lack of clarity and misunderstandings, potentially adding more problems and delays. Panic can also spread among team mates. Harnessing pressure to concentrate your mind on a problem, however, can elicit great results.

Staying power – and when to give up

The flip side to time pressure is when the problem takes ages to solve. In this case the challenge is to prevent a loss of interest, going stale or despondency. A key skill employers are keen to see is tenacity – the ability to keep working towards a solution until you achieve one, rather than giving up. And it's only by demonstrating staying power that you can be confident about giving up at the right time. As well as there being a place for persistence in problem-solving, you need to be able to cope when it's not possible to solve a problem. Effective evaluation of the situation will allow you to see when the most productive way forward is to give up. 'I do want problem-solvers who are resilient but I don't want them to keep flogging a dead horse,' comments a London-based IT manager. 'The ideal is the person who doesn't need to be told to start or stop – so has both initiative and good judgement about what's simply not worth pursuing.'

How you'll be tested on your problem-solving

Problem-solving may not be an explicit requirement set out in the job description, but it is likely to be tested in some way in most application processes – often at various stages, from application form to interview.

How you will be tested on your problem-solving will vary. You might be asked to tackle a hypothetical scenario, or you may be asked to give an example of when you have used a particular skill, for example using negotiation or initiative. At an interview, employers may pick an example you have given in your application form, asking you to elaborate on it. Pre-assessment centre screening may involve psychometric tests to look at your verbal and numerical reasoning (see Chapter 17). Ultimately, employers are gauging two things when it comes to problem-solving: your understanding of the skills they are looking for, and whether you possess them.

Demonstrating your skills: a problem-solving portfolio

A useful form of preparation is to pull together a mental 'problem-solving portfolio'. Employers want concrete and practical illustrations of your problem-solving experience, so it's really worth putting your mind to this now. Pick out a shortlist of examples that you can use to showcase your skills as fully as possible. The key is to think of examples that illustrate as many of the problem-solving skills we've discussed as you can, with good detail on the process and outcome. Quantifiable examples – how much money you saved, the mark you got – are helpful because they demonstrate an outcome clearly. It's also useful to try to find one example that brings in teamwork, so that you can show how you have problem-solved effectively working with others.

To include in your problem-solving portfolio:

- three different examples showcasing a variety of scenarios, each including two or three key problem-solving skills;
- a clear breakdown of the problem-solving steps;
- evidence of a successful solution.

What I found useful:

'Sometimes you really do just need to take the time to process something fully. I have found that I can get to the end of the day and a problem can have my mind in knots, and I can't see my way out of it. It really helps to try to switch off from the problem. Think about something else. Get a good night's sleep. And then return to it with more of a sense of perspective. Giving myself the chance to pause and be able to see the bigger picture definitely helps me work my way through a problem better.'

What I wish I'd known:

'No one has all the answers and often it is simply hard work and experience that makes people seem like they do a job effortlessly. I used to look at senior people in my profession and think they made it look so easy, but then I realized that practice and experience are key. Making mistakes is too, and I think I was far too nervous about making any. I wish I had been less afraid of making a mistake. Now I realize that making mistakes is often what we learn from the most.'

J.P. (Barrister)

Exercise

You're on holiday with a friend and your car breaks down in the middle of the countryside. Your barriers to solving the problem are that neither of your mobile phones works, you're miles away from any help and you're not able to fix the fault yourselves. Go through the six suggested problem-solving steps to work out a solution. Now imagine that your friend isn't happy with your plan. What do you do to resolve this so that you can implement your solution? At the end of the exercise, note each problem-solving skill you applied.

08
Industry knowledge

What is industry knowledge? It's being well informed and up-to-date on an area of work – from its history, how it's organized and the people it hires, to its challenges and future priorities.

When it comes to job hunting, industry knowledge consists of two main elements: your understanding of the industry you're looking to enter, and your understanding of the specific organization you are applying to. And, crucially, the two interlink. You need to be familiar with the ins and outs of the industry as a whole to understand where a particular organization fits in.

For your purposes – to be able to plan your career, seek out the best opportunities and succeed in the application process – you need to become an expert in the industry you're targeting. From an employer's perspective, your industry knowledge needs to persuade them that:

- your qualifications and experience would be an asset within the industry;
- your research and organizational skills have enabled you to gain a well-informed picture of the industry;
- your awareness and understanding of the industry and wider environment affecting it give you a competitive advantage.

Showcasing your industry knowledge

You'll be tested on your industry knowledge throughout the job application process, but it will often be down to you to be proactive about making the most of it. When it comes to your covering letter, for example, outlining how your interests and experience relate to the organization you are applying to will help to give your application relevance. Similarly, linking what you have learnt in your studies to current needs within the industry will also help to persuade employers that you would be an asset.

You'll most likely be applying for a number of jobs within your target industry, so a practical approach is to start by getting up to speed with an overview of the industry as a whole, then moving onto in-depth research on specific organizations each time you submit an application. It's worth emphasizing that what you don't have in industry work experience, you can, to an extent, compensate for with a good understanding of the industry, gained through careful research.

How well do you know your industry?

Are you interested in one particular industry or do your interests lie in several possibilities? If you are weighing up a few options, getting really familiar with each industry on your shortlist is essential for deciding what would suit you best.

Whether you're interested in one industry or more, to optimize your chance of getting into it your aim should be the same for each one: to get to know it inside out. Let's have a look at some of the key questions you need to be able to answer. The answers will vary considerably depending on the industry: a core part of building your industry understanding is working out the relevance of each question. You'll also find that you know some of the answers to the questions off-hand, but that others require investigation. One of the main purposes of going through these key questions is to get you to find your way around the industry while you seek out the answers.

An industry overview

Researching the answers to these questions will help you to put together a detailed picture of how the industry is organized and how it functions.

The industry landscape:

- How big is the industry? Is it small or large in size compared to other industries?
- How diverse is the industry? Does the industry divide into different sectors, for example with different specialisms, and how much variation is there in organization size?
- What influences are there on the industry? For example, what role do the economy, the law and politics play?

The main players in the industry:

- Which organizations are most important or influential in the industry? Does importance relate to size or to other factors?
- Who are the industry leaders and key influencers? What roles within the industry do they play?
- How do different organizations relate to each other in the industry? Do they compete with each other, work together or function independently?

The state of the industry:

- How well is the industry currently doing? Is it expanding or shrinking?
- What are the main priorities at the moment?
- How is the industry affected by new developments? For example, regulation, funding or technological changes?
- What challenges does the industry face?

Entry into and progression within the industry

Addressing these questions will help give you an understanding of who works within the industry and what opportunities there are.

Routes into the industry:

- Is there one main route in, or are there different options? How long does each route take? Is one route more highly regarded by employers than others?
- What qualifications are required to get into the industry? Is there a performance minimum for qualifications, such as a 2:1 bachelor's degree classification?
- What professional membership bodies does the industry have, if any?
- Is work experience essential, and if so in what form?
- How competitive is it to get into the industry? Is there a shortage or surplus of entrants?

Progression opportunities:

- What are the hierarchies in the industry? How do you move from one level in the hierarchy to another?
- How long do people tend to stay in the industry? What other industries do those leaving go into?

Pay and conditions:

- What are typical starting salaries?
- What is the basis for pay progression?
- Is there significant variation in pay across different organizations?
- What are typical working hours?

TIP: *Some industries currently have less diverse intakes than others, but this should never put you off. Increasingly, diversity and inclusivity are priorities for organizations right across sectors, and many industries are actively trying to broaden their intake. Check out campaigns/organizations that are working on diversifying the industry you're interested in. Advice and support are often on offer, as well as opportunities to be given mentoring.*

Where do you see yourself in five years?

This is a question that often comes up in interviews. Putting your mind to having an answer to this is a good way to demonstrate your knowledge of an industry's career progression opportunities, and it's also a useful way for you to reflect on the details of your longer-term career plan.

Getting industry expertise

Your research for answering the questions we've been looking at will take you from the websites of professional associations to those of government departments, via your careers service, the library and possibly sites like Wikipedia. Let's now look at some ways to go beyond the basic nuts and bolts of your industry and keep up to speed with it.

Industry publications

Reading industry-specific publications – from trade journals to annual reports to newsletters – is a great way to keep up-to-date on new developments, priorities and opportunities. For pay-to-read publications your local public library will stock many trade journals, and online publications such as quarterly magazines are now often free to download. Sign up to newsletters via email, and set up Google Alerts for organizations you're interested in to receive notifications on their activities, and also follow them on LinkedIn.

Following industry leaders on social media

Social media is a great way to get the inside scoop on what is happening in an industry. Choose a handful of leading and interesting people to follow in the industry. Twitter, LinkedIn and Facebook feeds, for example, will keep you informed about events and opportunities, issues affecting the industry, and on opinion and debate.

Industry blogs

Blogs, be they personal or 'official', allow you to follow discussions that are happening in the industry, revealing challenges that are being faced, views on news from the industry and often more informal insights into typical day-to-day life in the industry.

Industry role models

In many cases, part of why people are drawn to an industry is because they have been inspired by the passion and work of a particular person. Who has inspired you? Is there someone in the industry whose achievements you especially admire? What do you know about their career trajectory and their future aspirations? If you haven't got someone in mind, seek out some role models. Look at who writes the blogs you have found stimulating, think about who you've seen deliver speeches that were engaging and look up presentations and interviews on YouTube.

Attending industry events

In most industries there will be opportunities to attend events that are open to the public. As well as gaining insights into what is going on in the sector and hearing inspiring industry leaders, going to events is useful for networking opportunities. Keep up-to-date about upcoming events via newsletters and social media.

Keeping up with current affairs

It's not enough to know about the ins and outs of your target industry. You also need to know about what is going on in the wider world that might affect it. As well as keeping generally informed about what is happening in the news, keep abreast of how changing factors, from the global economy to national public policy, are impacting on the industry.

Work experience and internships

Being in the industry itself is one of the best ways to build up your knowledge and understanding. Make the most of any work experience opportunity by asking questions, attending events, making use of access to reports and publications, and seeking out recommendations for ways to get informed.

TIP: Set up an 'industry email' and use it to sign up to newsletters and receive Google Alerts. Keeping your industry research separate from your main inbox can help you to go through it more systematically.

Put an 'industry file' together

Don't wait to get familiar with your target industry until a job you're interested in comes up – get started now. As well as putting you in touch with opportunities, getting ahead on preparation avoids having to 'cram' at the last minute. Using the research you've already done to gain industry knowledge, put together an electronic 'industry file' for useful websites, downloads of relevant online publications, a list of blogs, profiles of industry leaders, pertinent newspaper articles and any industry contact details you have.

Industry knowledge and the job application process

Your key opportunity to demonstrate your industry knowledge is likely to be in an interview, but don't underestimate the chances to do so in your covering letter, application form and in assessment centre exercises. Throughout the application process your aim should be to demonstrate your understanding of how the organization you are applying to fits into the wider industry – and how your experience and qualifications fit into the organization's and industry's needs.

Having built up a foundation of general industry knowledge, then, when it comes to applying for a specific role, it's time to work on your knowledge and understanding of the organization you're applying for. Your first focus should be their website.

Website

Really study the website. You'd be surprised by how far this gets you and how frequently candidates don't do this properly. 'I am continually amazed by how little research candidates do about us before they come in for an interview,' comments a charity CEO. 'I can think of a number of recent examples when someone who is really good on paper will turn up to an interview unable to answer even basic questions on [the charity]. And it doesn't do them any good: there are lots of people trying to get into the sector, and I will always go for the person who gets it and has done their homework.'

What to look out for on the organization website:

Their people

- Know who the senior people are, the backgrounds of the founders, the number of people employed and the variety of roles. Pay attention to staff CVs, such as what they studied and which other organizations they've worked at before.

Their story

- Demonstrate that you are familiar with the organization's history as well as their latest developments. Make sure you know when and how the organization was set up, as well as any major changes such as mergers or takeovers.

Their ethos

- Does the organization have a particular philosophy or approach that guides its work? What is it and how does it distinguish it from others? Is the organization's ethos expressed in a motto or strapline?

Their main output: what they do

- Familiarize yourself with the organization's central focus, be it products, services, publications or other forms of output. What is their most important strand of work?

Their successes

- Look for any announcements of awards or other accolades, prominent clients or breakthroughs the organization has had.

Their latest news

- Through forums such as their blog, newsletter and social media, identify the organization's latest work, recent or upcoming events, latest achievements, recent developments and recruitment opportunities. Also look at the latest performance indicators where relevant, and where there is scope for comparisons, look at how their performance compares to previous periods.

Beyond the basics: wider research

You want to demonstrate to employers that you have taken the initiative to research the organization beyond the website. Having fully familiarized yourself with the basics, widen your research scope to look at what other people are saying about the organization. For example, look at write-ups about them on news sites, profiles on industry blogs and in trade journals, and service-user reviews. Look at profiles of their performance in comparison to other similar organizations. Who are the main competitors in the industry? Your grasp of the landscape in the sector is important, as well as your understanding of the role that competition plays. In business this might be described as your 'commercial awareness', but it applies in all contexts. For example, charities compete with each other for funding and education providers for students.

> **TIP:** Don't only talk about an organization's positives in your application. Showing awareness of the challenges they face, as well as discussing possible solutions, is a powerful way to demonstrate how informed you are.

The big industry knowledge interview question

'Why do you want to work here' is one of the most commonly asked questions in job interviews. Although it sounds almost frustratingly open-ended, employers ask it to elicit a number of key pieces of information about you: your research about and understanding of the organization and the wider industry; your motivations, enthusiasm and priorities; and your career aspirations. Your answer, therefore, provides an excellent opportunity to bring together and highlight your research and understanding of the organization, your industry knowledge and your own skills, interests and experience. A weak answer can give the impression not only of a lack of preparedness for the interview but also a lack of interest in the organization and industry. As such, you want to start thinking in detail about 'why you want to work here' from the moment you decide to apply for a job, spanning from your interest in the wider industry down to the specific role you are applying for.

In your answer, be sure to include:

- what, in your view, marks the organization out from others in the industry;
- how your background relates to the needs of the organization;
- how you see the particular role you are applying for drawing on your skills and contributing to the organization.

Interview questions
Bringing your knowledge of the industry
and the organization together

When you are preparing for a job interview you want to link your understanding of the industry as a whole to the specific organization you are applying to. Pick a leading organization that you are interested in and see if you can tackle the following questions:

- How does this organization compare to others in the industry?
- What measures of success are there in the industry, and how is your chosen organization performing against these?
- What factors have affected all organizations in the industry in recent years, and how have these impacted on your chosen organization?

And finally... ask the industry experts

In the chapter on communication skills we talked about the power of questions as a communication tool. Job interviews are one of the best opportunities you'll have to interact with people who work in the industry you're trying to get into – in other words, the experts. You can make the most of good questioning at the end of your interview by asking the interviewer how *they* stay abreast of developments and news in the industry. As well as being a good way to pick up insider tips, it demonstrates your engagement in the industry, your interest in getting more informed and your understanding that those on the inside of the industry have the greatest insight.

What I found useful:

'Every business is essentially a people business. Over the years, I have found it extremely useful to get to know people in different areas of the organization and to find out/understand what they do. This has proved helpful on a number of levels – it gives one a better sense of one's own position/role in the business, it helps one figure out which part of the business one is best suited to and, above all, when there are problems that need to be resolved, it means you know who to go to, you can engage with them better and you appreciate the challenges they face, as well as the ones you face.'

What I wish I'd known:

'Two things I have only come to fully appreciate in hindsight:

(1) Precisely because every business is a people business, there is always going to be a certain amount of politics in an organization. Recognizing this helps one to better gauge what is informing the actions around one and, in turn, helps to inform one's own actions. It's trite, but true: you can't please everybody all the time.

(2) Work isn't just about the 9 to 5 (or, in banking, the 7 "til you finish") – it's as much about the people you work with and the friends you gain.'

E.C. (Banker)

Exercise

In a couple of sentences, jot down an outline of your strengths as a candidate. Now imagine that you are applying for a job in your target industry and write a second outline of your strengths, linking them to the needs of the industry.

Finally, pick a leading organization in the industry and tailor the outline of your strengths to *also* include how they would serve that organization's goals and aims.

Part Three
Looking for a job

09
Systematic job hunting

If your job hunting is to be a success and the process a smooth one, it needs to be well organized. That means embarking on your job hunt with a solid plan of action, establishing a tightly targeted routine and having a clear set of priorities about the job you are after.

Although it can feel like it, job hunting isn't about luck; but it also isn't simply about being the best candidate on paper. The candidates who are successful don't only present themselves well and diligently complete lots of application forms, they also 'make their own breaks'. In other words, job hunting is about being proactive and creating opportunities as well as being methodical and focused.

What are you aiming for?

Your aim when you're job hunting is obvious: to get a job. It can be tempting to feel that you just need to get *a* job, but a key part of effective job hunting is making sure that you go beyond that basic goal and get a job that really suits your long-term aims and ambitions. But there's an important caveat to put in here: what this doesn't mean is that you should be under pressure to land your dream job right away. What we're talking about is finding a job that sets you on the path that takes you where you want to get to.

To ensure that you are finding and applying for the right jobs you need to sharply target your hunt. This is as much about looking for and fostering good opportunities as it is about being clear on what would suit you.

Your job-hunting criteria

To target your job search effectively you need to figure out which criteria you are seeking to fulfil. Although there will be overlap with your broader priorities, discussed in Chapter 2 in relation to career planning, the task here is to sharpen your priorities down to work out exactly which jobs you would consider. Your answers might relate to a preferred lifestyle as much as they do to career goals. For example, perhaps high up on the list of criteria you wish to fulfil is not having to work very long hours or take work home with you; or perhaps you want to live in a particular part of the country, so you need to find a job in that area. It's very likely that what you are looking for in a job will also relate to finding work in a specific industry; perhaps you are also keen to target a particular type of organization within that industry.

Start by making a list of the top five criteria you are hoping to fulfil in the job you secure. Once you've identified these, work out which three are your priorities, and then rank them in order. For example:

#1 A specific industry.

#2 A specific role in that industry.

#3 A workplace based in a particular geographical area.

Or:

#1 A higher than average starting salary.

#2 One or two specific industries.

#3 Opportunity to travel abroad.

Finally, work out whether any of these criteria are non-negotiable: in other words, factors that would make or break whether you considered a job.

Your elevator pitch

Having an 'elevator pitch' up your sleeve is an invaluable way to capitalize on chance meetings with people who might be able to help you get a job. Not just a trick for entrepreneurs, being able to sum up what you have to offer in a pithy and memorable way is a great asset to everybody on a job hunt. Come up with a couple of lines that summarize what you are looking for and what you have to offer. Try the lines on friends and relatives, and if you get the opportunity, try them on someone working in your targeted industry. Adjust your pitch according to any helpful feedback.

Your new job: job hunting

If you've now finished your studies and you're looking for a job, you've got a full-time one: job hunting. If you're nearing the end of your studies and trying to set yourself up with work, then you now have a part-time job: job hunting. Treating your job search like a job is the only way to do it systematically and invest the time required.

So, what does this new – full- or part-time – job look like?

The first thing to say is that it starts now: do not procrastinate. The sooner you get going, the further ahead you'll be. Next, set up a timetable: how long do you have to find a job? This will relate to when your studies finish, how long you are able to finance not working (more on this in Chapter 13) and how long you can afford to have a CV gap (for example, it's the summer after your degree has finished and you would like to get a job by September).

Having set a timetable, you now need to set up a weekly and daily schedule. These schedules are about making the most of the time you put into your job hunt, by taking a systematic rather than scatter-gun approach and setting a routine so you don't miss out on any opportunities. The overall aim is to make sure that every minute has a purpose and that you are not just aimlessly scanning the internet.

Where to look for a job

Half the challenge of finding a job is about looking in the right places and at the right time – and knowing how to seek out opportunities. The majority of jobs will be advertised, but you need to have a good plan to ensure that you are aware of what's being advertised. On top of that, some jobs *aren't* advertised, so you also need to ensure that you are creating opportunities for employers to find you.

Advertised jobs

Let's start by looking at how to target your advertised job search. The majority of advertisements are posted online, so where best to find them? Job sites are a key resource. These range from sites that advertise jobs across industries, to sites that are qualification and industry specific. Key general sites include Indeed, Totaljobs, Guardian Jobs, CV-Library and Monster, whereas Prospects.ac.uk, for example, is targeted at graduates and those with higher degrees, and Charity Job is a site specifically advertising non-profit jobs. Essential to sharpening your job search is identifying which sites – general and industry specific – advertise the types of role you are looking for. Make the most of sites that are relevant to your job search by:

- using filters on the site search to target the most suitable jobs;
- signing up for new job alerts to come straight into your inbox.

Jobs are also generally advertised on organizations' websites. It's common for an organization to advertise on both their own site and a job site, but don't bet on that. Rather than having to repeatedly check the sites of the organizations you want to work for, follow them on social media. Most will now announce openings through their Twitter and Facebook feeds, as well as on LinkedIn.

Recruitment fairs

Another key source of jobs is recruitment fairs, and these frequently target graduate job hunters. Recruitment fairs run up and down the country, throughout the year, so make sure you find out when ones near you – or relevant to you – are being held. Don't forget to also check what your own university or college has arranged.

Recruitment fairs provide a range of excellent opportunities and are also a great way to vary the routine in your job search. It's important that you don't get permanently stuck behind your computer during your job hunt and that you get out and meet employers. Recruitment fairs will allow you to find out about opportunities, pick up insider tips on getting jobs, have the chance to talk to and ask employers questions, meet recent graduate hires and network.

Maximizing what you get out of a recruitment fair does, however, require thinking ahead. Here are some tips on how to make the most of the opportunity:

- Plan your approach to the day well: keep an open mind about the employers you speak to but target your time well. This is as much about deciding which recruitment fair to go to as it is about which employer stand to seek out.
- Sign up as soon as possible: most fairs are free, but places can be limited.
- Make the most of any workshops or talks that are put on: from CV surgeries to careers advice, take up the chance to enhance your job hunt.

- Don't drift about at the fair: timetable your visit. What's on and which employers are there will be advertised, so jot down what you want to do and who you want to meet before you go.

- Prepare some key questions that you want to ask employers. This is a great opportunity to be able to ask things that you can't find out on their website or questions that relate specifically to your own background and experience.

- Bring your CV (several copies on paper and if possible, electronically on your phone or laptop) and practise your 'elevator pitch'. This way you're armed to seize any opportunity.

- Network! Try to speak to people, ask for employers' cards and exchange contact details where appropriate.

- Follow up on any interactions you have: if you met an employer and they gave you their details, send them a follow-up email the next day. There might not be a specific opportunity you are pursuing, but building up your contacts and networks is always useful.

Seeking out jobs

Not all jobs are advertised: sometimes because they are recruited for within an organization, or sometimes because people 'create' a job by presenting themselves as an excellent candidate ie by sending in a speculative application.

Speculative applications can lead to a role because the employer decides to take on a candidate even though there isn't an advertised vacancy, or because an employer puts an applicant forward for a vacancy they were unaware of or one that comes up in the future. There are of course no guarantees when you send in a speculative application; however, it can be something worth doing if there is an organization you are especially keen to work for that doesn't have any advertised opportunities. Some workplaces actively encourage speculative applications and state so on their website – but also beware that other workplaces explicitly refuse them, so make sure you check if they have a policy on this first.

A speculative application needs to really hit the mark to have effect – both in who it goes to and how well tailored it is. Carefully research whose attention you are trying to capture and make your covering letter as compelling as possible. Note what one employer in a highly competitive industry advises:

A lot of speculative applications that I get focus on the interests of the applicant rather than the needs of the organization. I would really recommend finding out exactly what an organization is trying to achieve and tailoring your potential contribution to that. Too often these speculative applications look like they have been fired off desperately to everyone under the sun.

Use your networks

Another way to seek out opportunities that are not advertised is by using your networks. You might not feel that you currently have an address book full of contacts, but you will have a wider network than you think. Do you have any professional contacts you can reach out to, explaining that you are looking for a job? Perhaps you did some part-time work or work experience with them in the past. Do you know anybody who currently works in the industry you're trying to get into? They may well have some inside knowledge about opportunities or could put you in touch with people in charge of recruitment. Your university/college is also a source of valuable contacts; as well as making the most of any help you can get from the careers service, many institutions have active alumni networks, which can be a great way to get advice and even introductions.

Social media for job hunting

Whether you have personal social media accounts, such as Twitter, or not, it's worth setting up professional ones as part of your job hunt. You can use social media to follow and reach out to employers, allowing you to keep abreast of job opportunities, let people know what roles you are looking for and ask employers questions. You can also post views on industry-related issues and repost relevant articles, showing employers who look at your feed that you are keeping up with the industry. Choose a profile picture that is professional, use your name as the handle for clarity, and keep your interactions and postings professional and relevant. You can use your profile on the platform to outline your credentials and the area of work you are seeking employment in. For more discussion on getting the most out of social media for career purposes, see Chapter 11.

A note on LinkedIn, currently the most popular professional social platform. Other professional social networks exist, and it's worth keeping abreast of what employers in your targeted industry use, but LinkedIn has so far proved to have the widest reach and longest staying power. It's definitely worth setting up a LinkedIn profile – essentially an online CV – so that you can connect with professionals (through link requests) and find and apply for jobs advertised through it. Put care into your LinkedIn profile when you set it up: it will often be the first thing employers see if they put your name into a search engine. Again, use a professional photo, use your 'elevator pitch' to put together a short and informative summary of yourself, keep your profile regularly updated, and pay attention to accuracy to avoid factual errors as well as typos.

Your job-hunting folders

To keep yourself organized make an electronic job-hunting folder that includes:

- your latest CV;
- any relevant grade transcripts;
- any relevant training certificates;
- referee details and any references that have been sent directly to you;
- all your applications (including advertisements and details for any jobs you've applied for);
- any job-hunting research you've gathered.

Also set up web-browser bookmarks for:

- job sites;
- your professional social media links;
- relevant organizations' job pages;
- your go-to job sites.

Making a success of rejection

When job hunting is your job, it can be difficult not to lose your enthusiasm at times. One thing to help keep up your morale is to remember that the process of job hunting *isn't* only a failure until you get a job. Every application that gets rejected is contributing to the endgame, giving you more experience, honing your application skills and ultimately getting you closer to success.

Getting rejected for a job is never going to be fun, but you can make the most of any lessons to be learnt from the experience, as well as any contacts you've made during the process. Each time you get a rejection, go over your job-hunting strategy: are you applying for the right jobs? For example, was that particular job really suited to your CV? Review your written application: could anything have been improved? How good is your covering letter, looking back at it? If you got to the interview stage, what could you have done better or differently? Were you sufficiently prepared? Are there any ways you think your skills or experience fell short? If so, what can you do to boost either?

Responding to the rejection

If your written application doesn't get to the next stage, you may not hear back from the employer: they will generally alert you to this in the job advertisement. If they do write to you with a rejection, be it in response to a written application or following an interview, it's important to respond well. Always write back thanking them for their time: showing courtesy is not only professional, it can also help keep you in the employer's mind for the future. If you have been interviewed, you should also ask for feedback. Remember that you are asking for a favour here: don't demand feedback and be clear about what you're asking. Rather than saying 'I'd like some feedback', ask politely if there is anything specific about your application, or your experience and skills, that you could improve. If you do get feedback, be sure to reply with thanks.

What I found useful:

'Job interviews are an opportunity for you to showcase yourself to the people who you'll work alongside if you're successful, so it's important that they get a sense of who you are and what you're about. It can sometimes be difficult to keep cool, calm and collected, especially when you are being asked challenging questions, but try not to be defensive. The interview is not an attack, so don't defend what you've done – explain it. Going to an interview with an "explanation" – not "defence" – mindset is something I've found really helpful. It helps with rejections, too: you'll likely know when a place is not the "right fit" for you.'

What I wish I'd known:

'CVs are not a one-time document. Instead, they can – and should – be tailored for the jobs you're applying to. Your CV should emphasize your skills and experience as they each relate to the specific tasks you'll be asked to undertake if you're appointed. Don't update your CV every six months. Update it with each application.'

S.Z. (University lecturer)

Exercise

Think of two people you know who have jobs they really love, in any industry. Find out how they got the job, asking them about how long it took to get it and what they were doing before, as well as what the application process entailed. How do their experiences compare with each other? What hints/tips can you take from their experiences to help your own job hunt?

10
Understanding what employers want

The whole concept of job-readiness centres on what employers want to see in recruits: the key ingredients that make for a strong employee. So far, we've talked a lot about the skills employers want; this chapter focuses on the attitudes, values and behaviours they want to see. In many respects, what we are looking at here are those qualities and attributes that exist 'between the lines': job advertisements often won't be explicit about seeking them, and it will frequently be their *absence* that raises issues for employers.

It's worth highlighting that your chance to demonstrate that you have the qualities that employers value isn't limited to your arrival in the workplace itself. The application process also provides good opportunities: from your self-awareness about the skills you don't yet have, to how faithfully you follow the application instructions, employers will be looking for the signs between the lines that indicate the type of employee you will be.

Your approach to work

Attitude

So, what do the characteristics and behaviours employers value look like? It might come as a surprise to hear how highly employers rate something as simple as having a positive attitude; for example: 'I'm not expecting a perfect employee especially when a new graduate starts, but having the right attitude counts for an awful lot. Someone who has a lot to learn but is coming in *wanting* to learn is on the track I want and the one that leads to success,' says an experienced management consultant.

Enthusiasm is a key part of this positive attitude employers are interested in: 'It really does make a difference if the employee behaves as though they actually want to be there,' comments a public affairs executive. 'You very quickly pick up when someone is more or less just biding their time before they can leave for the day, and if that's happening you've probably made a poor hiring decision.'

Having the right priorities is another aspect employers value in this regard. Bosses talk about desirable employees who are 'business aware' or 'customer focused': what they're referring to, and this applies to any industry, is an employee who prioritizes the needs of the organization. Perhaps this sounds like an obvious priority (you're on the right track if it does!); however, an employer complaint is that some employees do 'their' job in an isolated context. In this scenario the employee's priorities revolve narrowly around their particular responsibilities, rather than the overall objective of the organization. What employers want to see are staff who see themselves as part of the organization's overarching goal. A strong sense of purpose and productivity in a workplace requires everyone to be working towards the same core aim.

Values

It's a given that employers want to hire people whose values mean that the petty cash tin is safe, but as well as being able to literally trust employees, employers are looking for people they can go a step further with and actively *rely* on. From having been honest about your work experience on your CV, to keeping private any confidential information you have access to at work, employers want to hire people who will act with integrity. An employee with integrity can be depended on: you can take their word for what they say they have done and what they say they will do. Practically, this makes a big difference to employers – they don't need to keep monitoring you. As an employee you want your bosses to be able to rely on you because it means that they will feel able to give you more autonomy and responsibility, and thereby more opportunities and authority.

A strong work ethic

Few things are likely to trump a strong work ethic on an employer's list of desirables: an employee who is dedicated, works hard and has high expectations about their output is the hire you want to make.

Despite the term, a strong work ethic is more about action than a mentality, so what does it look like in practice? Here are some key characteristics employers point to:

- The employee is highly productive.
- They produce work that is consistent and of high quality.
- They get on with their work and don't procrastinate.
- They are disciplined, finishing rather than quitting tasks.
- They are focused and not easily distracted.
- They are dedicated, putting all their effort into their work.

A strong work ethic also denotes an employee taking responsibility for their work. This relates partly to high expectations and a sense of duty about producing work of a good enough standard. The other key component is about having the capacity to be self-reliant. This comes down to taking responsibility for your productivity, including taking the initiative when necessary rather than waiting to be told what to do.

Your work ethic isn't only demonstrated in how much effort you put into your own work; it also comes through in your approach to the work of others. Something that often comes up as a desirable trait is 'helpfulness'. Employers want staff who notice when help is needed – it could be carrying a pile of files, or it could be offering to step in for someone who is ill – and who don't need to be *asked* to help. Helpfulness is invaluable not only because it's useful in itself but because it shows that an employee can see where they can be useful and is prepared to put in that extra effort even if it's not 'their' problem.

The desire to develop

Connected to having a strong work ethic is being prepared to put the work into your development as an employee. One might think that employers want to hire candidates who know everything, but what is really valued are employees who want to learn and who put the time into doing so. One of the reasons for this is that learning employees are better 'investments': 'When I hire someone, I invest in them by training them up and I want a good return from that investment. I want them to be a better employee with a better skill set because they put their all into the training' (TV producer).

In practical terms, a willingness to learn is about taking up both formal opportunities – training that is on offer, for example – and informal opportunities – such as attending industry events and meetings where you can learn from your seniors. Learning new things isn't only about being open to the opportunity, it's also about getting good at identifying when one arises and then making the most of it.

Development doesn't stop at learning, of course, and actually applying what you have learnt to your work is essential. The application of what you've picked up, and the way that it improves your work, will often be how employers notice that you are putting time and effort into your development.

Continuous improvement is a central concept when it comes to learning in the workplace. In other words, learning and improvement is an ongoing process. This is as much about when as it is about how often. Don't imagine that learning and improvement is something only for newbies. Even the seasoned CEO has more to learn, as one such example, a well-established entrepreneur, emphasizes: 'You've gone wrong if you think you've ever completely cracked your job: there's always more to learn, and there are always ways to improve.'

Self-awareness: know your strengths and weaknesses

An essential tool to aid your continuous learning is practising self-awareness. You need to keep abreast of your strengths and weaknesses to be able to put your strengths to work and to work on your weaknesses. For example, if public speaking is something you feel uncomfortable with, you could consider this a current weakness to improve by taking up opportunities to practise it whenever possible. Equally, perhaps one of your key strengths is writing; if so, you want to really utilize this strength, so you might, for example, offer to contribute to the in-house blog.

Strengths and weaknesses MOT

List three strengths you could bring to a job and identify how you would put these to work in the job application process.

Next identify three weaknesses. If you've implemented improvement strategies for any of these, are they taking effect? For those weaknesses you haven't yet worked on, what could you do to help improve them?

Flexibility and adaptability

The flexible employee who is able – and crucially, willing – to adapt is the opposite of the one likely to say: 'I'm not doing that, it's not my job.' As well as being part of a mentality that enables you to develop as an employee, adaptability enables you to progress up the hierarchy. From a promotion perspective, for example, demonstrating that you can adapt to new tasks will help employers to see that you have the capacity to take on new work and greater responsibility. Your willingness to be flexible and to adapt also comes back to the idea of being an employee who can be relied on. This relates partly to the idea of helpfulness but also to an employee's prioritizing of the organization's overall goal. Crises are an example of times when flexibility is most useful: employers will want to ask those employees they can trust to take on a challenge.

Alongside all these characteristics that demonstrate your desire to develop, you do also need to recognize what you *can't* do. Your ability to judge what you can achieve strongly relates to being able to judge when saying no is necessary – and is intrinsic to being a reliable employee.

Ambition

Ambition often gets a bad rap, conjuring up images of the employee who will do anything to get ahead, regardless of who and what it involves trampling on. In reality, however, ambition is a vital ingredient of a good employee. Ambition acts as a personal motivator for you to excel in your job, and it shows employers that you have a desire to progress. Ambition also gives you direction: it helps you to formulate a career plan as you map out where you are striving to get to. Employers want to hire ambitious people, because employees with drive strive to succeed for their own purposes, not simply to fulfil their boss's expectations and earn their keep – which makes a boss's life easier. 'I think that ambition needs to be really championed in the workplace,' comments a gallery director. 'I want ambitious people working for me, otherwise I need to be the one putting all the effort into motivating them!'

Good organizational skills

As well as being imperative to efficiency, being organized is something every employee can – and should – achieve.

The basics of being organized include:

- punctuality;
- adhering to deadlines;
- keeping good systems for organizing your work and knowing where things are;
- being prepared eg for meetings and catch-ups;
- prioritizing what needs to be done.

Why being organized matters so much to employers is because of the negative impact of disorganization. For example, the employee who always turns up late is the one more likely to keep a client waiting and potentially lose their business. The employee who keeps missing deadlines is the one who is more likely to fail to get a document to a client on time, again risking losing their business. The employee who can never find anything is more likely to be the one who arrives at a meeting missing a vital document. It's all too common to think that what really matters is your 'actual work', rather than the process involved in doing it, including how organized you are. But as we've noted, a lack of organization can in fact actively thwart your output and lower your productivity, as well as that of others working with you.

The role of respect

What helps you work well with other people links strongly to the interpersonal skills we discussed in the chapters on teamwork and communication skills. Alongside these skills there are approaches to how you work with colleagues that can really enhance relationships, both maximizing efficiency and helping to avoid conflict. Employers want to see people who work constructively with colleagues and who diffuse rather than ignite disharmony.

Just as respect is a fundamental element of personal relationships, it's vital that you treat your colleagues with respect. Doing so doesn't mean that you have to agree with their opinions, or that you can't disagree about how to approach a piece of work. It means listening to and engaging with their ideas and views and responding in a manner that is courteous and constructive. On a more basic level, respecting people's different backgrounds and beliefs is a core tenet of behaving in a fair and professional way.

When there is conflict, showing respect becomes more, not less, impor-tant. For example, if you are angry that a colleague has behaved without integrity – let's say they've unjustly taken all the credit for a success – for the confrontation to be constructive, rather than destructive, you need to main-tain the level of civility that acting respectfully affords.

It goes without saying that your seniors in the workplace also need to be treated with respect. As well as applying the rules of engagement we've just discussed, you need to respect the decision-making authority your bosses have. Again, this does not mean having to refrain from offering a difference of opinion (courteously) or alternative solutions; it means understanding and accepting who makes the final decision.

When things go wrong

It's crucial to recognize that even the stellar employee with all the attributes we've been discussing *is* sometimes going to screw up. It's obviously worth doing everything to avoid this. Many of the qualities and behaviours we talked about, from honesty to setting boundaries, are precisely aimed at enabling you to be realistic and to foresee potential issues. But you also need to be able to handle situations where things have gone wrong in a way that is as productive as possible.

The good news is that employers will judge you on your overall record rather than when things go wrong – you're human, and if you have demon-strated to them that you have a good approach to your work, the issue will not be taken as indicative of a wider problem.

We talked about being honest earlier, and one of the most important things about limiting the damage of screwing up is not covering it up. There is no question that, as the saying goes, the cover up is worse than the crime. If making a mistake ends up revealing you to not have integrity, because you tried to hide it, that then becomes the issue, not the error you made in the first place. We've also talked about the importance of being ready to learn, and this too applies to understanding what went wrong and learning rather than hiding from your mistakes.

Finally, as well as learning from them you need to be able to move on from mistakes. Resilience is a word that often comes up in relation to being adaptable. An example of where being able to adapt to circumstances will serve you best is, first, dealing with something that has gone wrong and, then, accepting that it happened and moving on.

What I've found useful:

'Be likeable. I've always tried to build good relationships with my employers and colleagues by being approachable, open-minded and friendly, while maintaining professional boundaries. You don't have to be everyone's best mate, but I now know from being on the other side of the table and interviewing enough people, that I'd rather employ someone slightly less qualified who I know will gel and get on easily with others in the team, rather than someone who ticks all the boxes on paper but is quite frankly, "unlikeable".'

What I wish I'd known:

'Looking back, and even today, I see that it's important to know that only you can stand up for yourself and know your own worth. You are going to meet a lot of lovely and helpful people on your career path, but there will also be a few bumps in the road and people that either want to see you fail or have their own issues and try to put you down. Try not to be too sensitive or intimidated. It's natural to feel that way but it's not your problem, it's theirs. So be brave, be yourself, have integrity and confidence in your own abilities.'

B.C. (Civil servant)

Exercise

Put yourself in the shoes of an employer: imagine that it's your last day of your course and you have the luxury of hiring someone to help you move out of your halls of residence. Your recruit will be helping you pack up your room and move your things into a van, and they will drive you to your new accommodation. What skills and qualities would you like them to have? Out of these, what would be essential and what would be desirable? What negative qualities would stop you hiring them?

11
Social media, personal branding and self-promotion

Branding and promoting yourself may not sound like something you would naturally envisage doing. Yet the rise and scope of social media has provided a highly accessible opportunity to give your professional profile a head start. Using social media to establish a professional brand for yourself is an increasingly valuable way to impress employers. Employers not only value candidates who are well versed in a communications tool so widely used in the workplace today, they now often draw on social media content as an additional source of information about the type of employee you would be.

In this chapter we'll look at what constitutes your personal professional 'brand' with a view to focusing on how best to capture it across social media platforms, from Twitter to Facebook. Your first goal will be to identify what you want to convey through your brand, and your second, to implement a hands-on social media strategy to enable you to do this.

What is your social media brand?

Let's start by looking at what makes up your brand. When we talk about personal branding in this context, we're simply referring to building a professional reputation for yourself. This reputation is based on the key parts of who you are – your background, including your education and experience, your interests and passions, and where you are striving to get to. Social media provides you with a way to extract the essence of what you have to offer and put forward a dynamic showcase to complement your CV. What this means is that alongside your skills and achievements on paper, you also have the chance to add some insight into:

- how you present yourself and your work;
- how well you communicate and interact with others;
- your engagement with and knowledge of your target industry;
- your priorities and interests.

Your brand presented through social media, therefore, is an insight into your professional persona that you get to actively convey through the opportunities that social media platforms provide. Your goal in how you present your professional self is to showcase your strengths and what you have to offer by implementing effective social media strategies that will help promote you to prospective employers.

Brand management

Why social media offers job-hunters such a good opportunity is because it provides an unprecedented way to get people's attention. This means that you not only have the chance to connect with employers, but you also have the chance to give employers more information on the kind of candidate you are. Our focus is on maximizing the benefits of social media. But before we get there, let's make sure you first avoid the pitfalls.

How employers use your social media posts

So how do employers use your online presence in their decision-making? It's claimed that at least two-thirds of employers look you up on the internet before deciding whether to invite you to an interview. Why? Because they want to see if they can add anything to their picture of you garnered through your CV, covering letter or application form. This makes sense: employers need as much information as possible to help them choose the best person for the job, and your digital footprint potentially provides them with a great source of extra – unfiltered – 'intelligence'. This supplementary information hunting is partly about wanting to discover more about your broader pro-file, but it's also about vetting you. Is there anything out there that raises alarm bells for employers?

   In short, what you do – and have done in the past – online can help or hinder your chances of employers taking your application further. And it is social media in particular that is your friend or foe in this. Social media platforms allow you to highlight your skills and achievements, but what you put on them can also lead to employers making negative decisions about you. 'Brand management' when it comes to promoting your professional profile is therefore as much about making sure you don't sabotage yourself as it is about making sure you promote yourself effectively.

Cleaning up your existing online act

So, before you go any further, you may need to tidy up your online act.

These days most of us have at least something of a digital footprint. Start by Googling your name and seeing what comes up. What you find might look something like this: that under-11s athletics trophy you won at primary school, reported in the local newspaper; perhaps a donation to your friend's sponsored cycle ride across Wales; any social media posts you've written or shared; and any pictures you've posted.

Assuming you haven't been involved in a widely reported scandal, the potential booby traps of your online footprint tend to lie in your social media activity. If you have social media accounts that allow anyone to see your activity, is there anything on them you would rather not share with an employer? The things you'll be looking out for range from online swearing to compromising photos, including ones you are 'tagged' to. But keep in mind that you're not just seeking to edit out the shock factor: whether it's endless tweets about your latest celebrity crush or complaints about how totally bored you are killing time in a part-time job, think about how this extra information is going to affect your brand in the eyes of an employer. Even if your social media accounts are innocuous, it is worth remembering that mindless content that doesn't present a very flattering picture of your interests and use of time, can also act as a disadvantage.

If there are things that you think present a picture of you that may be less than helpful, you have a number of options:

- Change your settings to make your social media accounts private, and keep them as your 'personal' accounts.
- Delete any compromising posts and questionable photos and sort out any unwanted tagging where possible.
- Delete your personal social media accounts with a view to setting up new accounts to replace them.

Your aim when you go through your social media activity is a spring-cleaning exercise: putting things away and getting rid of anything unsuitable.

Building your social media strategy

Now we've got the clean-up out of the way, let's think about exactly what you are trying to do with your professional social media presence. Your goal is to build up a professional brand to enhance your opportunities, so what should your plan of action look like in detail?

Aim to:

- build a professional online profile;
- get people to notice your profile and engage with the content you post;
- use your content as a way to showcase your skills and experience;
- use social media as a digital business card by giving out your usernames or 'handles', as networking tools;
- network remotely with social media: connect with relevant industry people and establish relationships online;
- use social media as a way to help you stay informed and abreast of what is being said and done in your industry, including job opportunities.

Let's now look at what launching your professional brand on social media involves.

Picking your platforms

Picking your platforms is about choosing which social media will suit your output best, as well as making sure you have enough time to dedicate to your accounts. Your choices should be made on the basis of which forms of social media lend themselves best to your aims. This is both about what type of content is shared – for example, Instagram works well for pictures and Twitter for words – and about who uses the platform. Is a particular platform especially popular in your target industry?

You also want to make sure you don't spread yourself too thinly by having too many different social media accounts. Ideally you want to really focus your attention on one platform, so that you can dedicate time to maximizing the effectiveness of your online activity. Focusing on one type of social media allows you to get really familiar with the tricks of the trade, as well as your target audience. One option, if you don't want to limit your activity to a single platform, is to have a main social media outlet and cross-post with another.

Choosing your usernames/handles

Are you going to build up an existing social media account or are you going to set up a new one? The advantage of building up existing accounts is that you probably already have some content and followers. The potential disadvantages, as we discussed, revolve around posts that are inappropriate or irrelevant for professional purposes. If you do set up new accounts, always go for usernames, or handles, that clearly identify you and are professional, ideally based on your name and surname.

Putting together a good profile

Your profiles on social media need to be short, so stick to a vital information approach that's presented in a succinct way. Specify your educational background and your target industry, and highlight any specific interests within the industry. It can be worth including an email address in your biography to make it as easy as possible for people to get in touch. As the email address will be public, don't use your main email account as it will make it vulnerable to Spam. Do also include a photograph of yourself in your profile: you are more likely to get followers and responses if people are sure it's an account belonging to a real person. As with your LinkedIn profile, discussed in Chapter 9, choose a professional-looking photo, preferably a simple headshot.

Posting with purpose

Carefully curate your social media content, by posting, interacting and sharing with purpose. Your ultimate aim is to promote what you have to offer, through examples of work that you've done, your engagement with your target industry and insight into your priorities. So, for example, if you have written a blog, you can highlight this by posting a link to it. If you attend an industry event, posting perceptive comments about it will show that you're getting experience of the industry and that you understand it well enough to offer informed views on it. If you've raised money for a charity, posting about why you've fundraised for them (ie why you think their work is important) showcases your values as well as your fundraising skills.

Aim for a rough balance between posting your own content and sharing that of others. Keep in mind that generating your own content can simply involve posting a view on a relevant issue: you don't need to have a piece of work to showcase. Enhance what you share by always adding a comment that highlights why you think it's worth sharing.

To interact with and get noticed by people in your industry of interest, try to join in with conversations as well as starting them up. Spot opportunities for conversations by following the professionals and organizations most relevant to where you're trying to get to. Follow up with professionals you meet by connecting with them on social media. It's also useful to build on as many existing links as possible. Follow your university/college, any work places you've been employed by or done work experience at, and any charities you support. Linking your profile and posts with theirs can lead to your content being reposted by them and potential follow-up.

Is having lots of followers important? No. It will take time to build up a professional social media following, and don't be discouraged if you don't ever get to particularly large numbers. Remember that your aim is to present your professional brand online, rather than rule the social media world. Many of the people you want to view your social media output or interact with – employers in particular – won't follow you, but they may check out your digital profile or respond to your messages.

> **TIP:** *Be sure about what you're sharing. For example, don't share articles if you've only scanned the headline: you might end up inadvertently sharing content that you didn't intend to.*

Set a routine

Set up a social media routine and commit to it. Using social media consistently is much more effective than randomly blitzing it one month and ignoring it the next. You need to invest time into your social media in order to:

- keep content coming;
- stay abreast of activity and news from those you follow, including job opportunities;
- reply to messages/comments;
- join in conversations;
- spot new accounts worth following.

It's a good idea to schedule your social media activity into your week, for example, dedicating 15 minutes each morning to it, so that you do invest the necessary time. An allocated social media session is also a good way to not find yourself taken over by social media. Whether it's constantly checking the number of likes you've had on a post or trawling the internet for something – anything! – that you can share, social media needs to work for you, rather than you becoming enslaved to it. Stick to your time slot and work through a checklist that allows you to steadily keep building your online profile. Another reason for taking a timetabled approach to social media is the importance of careful posting when you're trying to build a professional brand. Don't get too casual and cavalier: only share content from credible sources, watch out for typos and spelling mistakes, and keep your tone professional.

> **TIP:** *Beware that humour is especially vulnerable to misinterpretation on social media. Always be cautious about posting amusing remarks on your professional accounts.*

Keep up your brand

Using social media to promote your brand isn't just about putting your professional profile out there during a job search. Once you're in a job, a strong social media brand is a great asset, potentially leading you to opportunities, keeping you up to speed with relevant discussions, adding weight to your industry reputation and helping you to build up your networks. 'These days there isn't a single graduate role we recruit for that wouldn't benefit in some way from having the online presence of an active Twitter account,' notes a recruitment consultant. 'In my view, social media isn't really optional anymore – if you're not using it to connect and communicate you're failing to utilize a tool that you straightforwardly can't afford to miss out on.'

All the opportunities social media gives you as you look for a job, from showcasing your strengths to engaging with people in your targeted industry, continue to have value as you work your way up the career ladder. To go back to our starting point, the professional brand that you can capture and capitalize on through social media is one you can continue to develop and adapt as your targets and priorities evolve.

What I found useful:

'When you post on social media, I believe it's important to have the courage of your convictions and to stand up for what you believe in. However, I would argue that one should choose one's battles. If you are seen to be continually ensconced in heated debate with people on a particular issue, or multiple issues, this could lead others to suspect that you may not be a team player or that you may be disruptive. It's also worth remembering when you engage in such debates – are you regularly doing this during working hours? If you are, an employer is unlikely to view this favourably.'

What I wish I'd known:

'Social media can take over every minute of your day and night if you aren't careful. While connecting you to the many millions around the world, it can potentially leave you feeling incredibly isolated. Employers will likely also take note of how you regulate your social media posts and their quantity and quality. Don't just post for the sake of posting. That could have a negative effect on how you are perceived by potential employers. You want to send out a clear message that you use technology proactively and productively, rather than to procrastinate. Not being on social media all the time also indicates that you're able to maintain a balance between your private and professional life.'

S.W. (Press and PR manager)

Exercise

Find three social media users in an industry you're interested in, on three different platforms. How are they using social media to enhance their profile in the industry, in your view? Which posts are particularly engaging and which ones less so? How does the different platform affect the effectiveness of their social media use? Does one platform work better than another, overall?

12
Networking

In this chapter we'll look at the two key pillars of networking: building up your networks and maximizing the effectiveness of the networking opportunities you secure. Over previous chapters we've touched on many scenarios in which you are developing your networks. For example, you are networking when you organize work experience by contacting organizations in your target industry, and you are networking when you talk to employers at careers fairs during your job hunt. And you are of course networking when you make professional connections via social media. We've also touched on many of the skills you put to use during a networking opportunity, from effective questioning to optimizing information gathering. In other words, the world of networking is one that you have already started work on, and one in which you are further ahead than you may think.

The purpose of networking

So, what is the point of networking in the professional world? Ultimately, networking is about making professional connections to gather information on and gain insights into an industry, and to make contacts. When you are looking for a job, networking is a key tool for putting yourself in the best possible position for employment by helping you to:

- make connections with employers and make yourself known;
- make links that allow you to get to know people who work in the industry;
- find out about potential opportunities and jobs;
- find out as much as possible about your industry of interest and particular organizations;
- get advice on ways into an industry or a particular role;
- get tips on how to tailor your applications most effectively;
- secure work experience opportunities.

Two things are worth keeping in mind about networking. The first is that chances to network don't all look the same, and one of the skills of effective networking is being able to identify good opportunities. You might automatically think of networking as being about attending events with lots of delegates, but if you are doing work experience and have occasion to ask an employee about how they got into their role, that can also be networking.

The second pointer is not to make the mistake of thinking networking is a one-way process. Especially when you're starting out in your career, networking is often seen as a way of getting people to help you – by introducing you to others, giving you tips and alerting you to opportunities. But to be really effective, networking should be a two-way process. As well as seeking connections and information that will enhance your career prospects, you also have something to offer: yourself. While you are networking you should be putting yourself forward as a highly employable candidate. The way to do this is by making connections in a way that impresses employers, both so that they keep you in mind for opportunities, and so that they are keen to connect you with colleagues because they can see you would be an asset. It is worth remembering that when industry insiders connect or recommend you to others, they themselves are networking by putting forward someone they think has promise.

Making the most of every networking opportunity

Before we look at the networks you already have and how to build these up, let's look at how you can maximize your networking potential by establishing a pre- and post-networking routine. This is about approaching each networking opportunity with a defined goal, and then following up effectively.

Start by defining what you are planning to network for: what are you trying to find out and who are you trying to meet? For example, are you at the point where you are trying to get into a specific role in an industry and therefore want to meet the people who can help you achieve this? Or are you at the point where you are exploring an industry, or perhaps more than one, and want to get more familiar with the opportunities available? The next stage of working out your networking goals is to identify what specifically you hope to get out of interactions with industry insiders. With a clear remit for what you are trying to find out you can target your networking much more successfully.

To capitalize on each networking opportunity, you need to have a good follow-up system. For every connection you make and every conversation you have, keep records of what you have found out and any lines of follow-up, be they contact details or suggestions for people to reach out to or articles to read. And always follow through with the tips or contacts you are given – failing to do so completely undermines the purpose of your networking.

The other imperative aspect of networking follow-up is thanking people for their time and help, where appropriate. Whether it's a cup of tea with your next-door neighbour or a meeting with the CEO of a top organization in your target industry, never forget to acknowledge their help and express your gratitude. Not only is it basic courtesy, following up with a thank you email can be a good way of keeping the connection going. How you behave plays a key role in the impression you leave on potential employers and those who might recommend you. Your aim should be to impress them when you network, with informed questions, a professional approach and good manners; don't alienate them by not knowing enough, asking too much or failing to appreciate their time.

Identifying your existing networks

Everybody has networks. Although you might think that networking is the preserve of high-flying executives, you've actually already spent a good deal of time developing networks. So, the first thing you need to do is work out who is in your personal network, those links and relationships you've built over the course of your life. You'll have informal networks (friends, family, neighbours, people you used to babysit for) as well as more formal networks (school and university/college contacts – staff and students – and any other institutional connections you have, for example, through a voluntary role or part-time job).

The purpose of identifying who you already know in each sphere of your life is to work out whether you have any connections that might help you career-wise. A good way to go about joining up any relevant dots is by going back to your networking goal and then working out whether anyone you know might be helpful. So, for example, as a starter, if you want to find out about how to get into a particular job, do you know anyone in that role? Or perhaps you know someone who doesn't do the job itself but works in the same industry, so therefore may well know someone who does.

Your university/college links can also be a source of networking potential. Universities and colleges often have active alumni networks, as discussed in previous chapters, that can be a great way to widen your connections. Some universities also offer mentors; for example, recent graduates in your degree subject, who can offer career advice and help you to connect with people they know.

> **TIP:** *When using personal connections, it's important to apply the standard thank you rules. This isn't just about showing your appreciation to friends or family members, it's also about ensuring they have confidence that you won't undermine professional relationships they connect you to by not behaving professionally yourself.*

Fostering industry opportunities to network

Now you've started putting your personal networks to work, let's think about how to build up a professional network within your targeted industry. This is about identifying ways to connect and meet professionals with whom you don't already have a link.

The main ways to build your industry networks include:

- approaching organizations for work experience;
- attending industry events, including conferences, trade fairs, speeches and networking events;
- attending recruitment fairs;
- joining professional associations in order to attend their events and capitalize on their networks;
- requesting 'informational interviews' in which to ask employers for advice;
- connecting with industry insiders through social media, for example, LinkedIn, as discussed in Chapter 11.

The first thing to do in building your industry network is to go back to your networking goals and identify which of the routes listed above will help you to achieve them. Each of these networking scenarios presents you with potential opportunities to interact with employers and those working in the industry. Simply interacting with people, however, is not enough: the next step is to arm yourself with the necessary tools and information to be able to turn interactions into effective networking opportunities.

Effective networking: events

Industry events come in many different forms, including conferences, seminars, lectures, product launches and trade shows; and they provide excellent opportunities to interact with those working in the industry. Whatever type of event it is, there is generally a chance to mingle – and herein lies your chance to network.

For your interactions to be successful, you need to go into them fully prepared. So, before you attend an event do the following:

- Carefully research the event's focus: you want to be able to make informed conversation about it with other attendees.
- Find out who is going to be there: for smaller and medium-sized events an attendance list is often emailed around, so look up some of the attendees' online profiles. Being aware of recent work they have done, and knowing about the organizations they work for, can be very useful for starting up conversations.
- Identify 'targets': depending on how much you are able to find out about attendees, identify individuals you would like to try to speak to.
- Have some opening lines up your sleeve for people you want to meet. For example, 'I wanted to say how much I enjoyed your recent article on x.'
- Come up with an introduction: in a single, punchy line how are you going to give yourself the best shot at engaging with people? Think about what basic information you need to include when you introduce yourself and what details will be most relevant to the industry people you are likely to meet at such an event.
- Make sure you are up to speed with what is going on in the industry, as well as on current affairs. A key part of networking in person, just as on social media, is about being able to join a conversation, so make sure you can participate in topical discussions.

For each of the prep steps set out above you need to have your networking goals in mind – from how you introduce yourself to who you target. Tailoring each approach to your aims will make your interactions much more fruitful.

When it comes to the event itself, apply the following five basic principles to help you get the most out of being there:

1 Always find someone to speak to – whether it's going up to one of your 'targets', approaching someone standing alone, or joining a group; make sure you interact as much as possible.

2 Start every interaction by briefly introducing yourself – use your industry-tailored introduction.

3 Listen – don't spend too long talking about yourself or inadvertently switch off while you wait for a gap in which to ask a prepared question.

4 Don't monopolize people – part of good networking is not overstaying your welcome and recognizing when people want to move on.

5 Follow up with everyone you meet – maximize the potential of every interaction by following up with an email if you've been given contact details, and on social media if you haven't.

Effective networking: informational interviews and one-to-one meetings

One-to-one meetings with those working in your target industry can be invaluable sources of advice, connections and even opportunities – if you set yourself up for them well. Whether it's an informational interview with an employer – where you get the chance to ask for advice, for example, on getting into the industry – or whether it's a more informal chat over a coffee with an industry insider, being fully prepared is essential.

Good preparation for one-to-one meetings is about ensuring that you get the most out of it by having a clearly thought out and well-defined aim. Before the day of your meeting, make sure you've done your homework. You don't want to waste any time asking questions you could have found the answers to on the organization's website, and you want to capitalize on the opportunity to get an insider's informal perspective. You also want to make sure that the person you are meeting thinks that your questions are worthwhile. You are aiming to give them a good impression, and how well you utilize the meeting will give them an insight into how you approach your work.

When the meeting starts, it's helpful to begin by finding out how much time the person you are seeing has available for you. This indicates both that you understand the value of their time and will also help you to prioritize your questioning accordingly. Next, briefly summarize your education, work experience and career goals, going on to specify what advice you are after. Outlining exactly what you are trying to get out of the meeting will make it more productive, as the industry insider will have a better idea about what to focus on. Ideally, you will have been clear about what you want to discuss in your initial phone or email approach, but it's always worth reiterating at the meeting itself. The other practical point to add is to bring a pen and notepad and write down any advice you are given. Not only will this help you remember what you need to for follow-up, it will show that you are taking the meeting seriously and making the most of the thought being put into answering your questions. Finally, when the meeting finishes, be sure to say thank you and follow this up with an email.

> **TIP:** Don't ask for too much: for example, if at an informational interview an employer suggests you get in touch with a particular organization, unless the employer offers to provide contact details, show initiative and find them out for yourself.

Network for others – and into the future

Many opportunities that come through for you will be thanks to people giving up their time and expertise to help you, be it by giving you tips over a cup of coffee or by introducing you to a colleague via email. Be sure to follow this example by doing what *you* can to help others network. For example, where you have a personal connection in an industry your course mate is trying to get into, try to make an introduction. Or if a younger family friend is interested in applying to the university or college you studied or are currently studying at, offer to have a chat with them about your experience there. Helping other people to network isn't just about building good karma. It's also about getting into a mindset where making connections with people becomes second nature, an outlook that will serve you well throughout your professional life.

Networking is something you will continue to do all the way through your career. Networks will help keep you up to speed with opportunities in your industry, link you to the people you need to know, familiarize you with your competitors and enhance your professional profile. Never underestimate how valuable knowing people is, and put time and effort into keeping your networks dynamic by staying in touch with contacts, introducing them to others and keeping them abreast of your work. And aim for a wide-ranging contact book by not limiting your networking solely to your industry. One day the web designer you met at a dinner party or the accountant you met at a fun run may be just the person you need in your professional life.

What I found useful:

'You've got to know someone's background and find a point of common interest when you're networking – people aren't interested in you, they want to talk about themselves, so do your background research, find something that you could build a conversation around and share information accordingly. Networking is essentially a value exchange. If you're meeting someone cold, ask them what they are working on and go from there.'

What I wish I'd known:

'I wish I'd realized sooner that when it comes to networking, simply being enthusiastic only works for so long. It's that old adage: what got you here won't get you there. As you get further into your career, you need to step up your game when it comes to networking. Email introductions are a good example. If you want an introduction, make it as easy as possible for someone to introduce you by laying out something they can quickly copy and paste about who you are, why you're interested in connecting and when you are available (and if making an introduction, always check with both parties first!).'

E.H. (CEO, Fashion tech start-up)

Exercise

Draw up a table that includes columns for family, friends, family friends and neighbours. With your target industry in mind, list those in each column who might have a link to it. The link may be direct, or it might be that you know they have a friend or relative themselves in the industry. If you succeed in coming up with a link to your target industry, with your networking goals in mind, plan and then make an approach.

13
Budgeting and money skills

Budgeting and money skills will make life easier at every point in your life: whether you're still at university or college, job hunting or starting a new job. Being on top of your finances – from how much money you have, to how much you are spending – makes a huge difference, not just to your peace of mind but also to the opportunity and freedom you have to pursue what you want to do. Getting into financial difficulty, on the other hand, can be hugely restricting, as well as stressful.

When you start a new job, you want to be in a well-organized and stable financial position rather than chaos. Beginning your career with money problems can limit your options, distract you from your overall goals and negatively affect your performance at work. Money problems very quickly take their toll, and creating an orderly financial life is an essential investment in guarding against them.

In this chapter we'll look at the approach, strategies and skills that will help you to manage your money well, from how to make the most of what you have, to the money traps to avoid. The theme running through the chapter is taking care of your money by being systematic and shrewd in equal measure. Ultimately, managing your finances well is about getting familiar with your money as much as it is about being on top of your financial admin.

Value every penny

The first step of good money management is getting into the right mentality about your money: 'Look after your pennies and the pounds will take care of themselves' is the financial motto you want to live by. Why? Because being careful with your money is the key to financial security. Too many of us don't know what we have, how much we are spending, what we are buying and where all our financial information is. The result is that we're unable to plan ahead, save or make sound decisions about our money, meaning we end up wasting it.

So, let's start with a key question: how much money do you have right now? You'd be surprised by how many of us aren't really sure – or perhaps that also goes for you at the moment. Ideally you should be able to be close to exact about how much money you have at any given time, and the way to do this is to get on top of your money once and for all.

Review and organize your financial life

The second step to getting to grips with your money is to put together an up-to-date record of every detail of your financial affairs. Think of your financial life as falling into four main categories:

- income ie how much money you have coming in;
- spending;
- savings;
- debt.

We'll go on to examine your spending shortly, but first, let's organize your financial information so that you have it all in one place. This task is about working out how your money fits into each of the four main financial categories above.

Get a pen and paper, or open up a blank Word file, and write down:

- your current account(s) details (bank name, account number and sort code) and the amount of money in it/them;
- your savings account(s) details (again, bank/building society name, account number, etc) and the amount of money in it/them;
- any debts: the details of any overdraft facility you are currently using, any loans (excluding student finance loans, which we'll discuss later in the chapter) and credit card balances;
- any other money you have, for example, in the form of gift vouchers, as well as cash.

WARNING! Keep these notes safe, whether they're in a notebook or on your computer. See box below for tips on protecting your sensitive information.

Work out how much you currently have, minus any money you owe. The next step is to start a money log, using the information discussed above. You can do this any way you will find easiest to update, for example as a folder on your phone. The aim is to always have to hand a record of what money you have, and what debt you have, and where. Don't keep any passwords for your online accounts in the same place as your account details, and preferably keep all passwords encrypted (again, something you can do on most smartphones and with most banking apps). Do, however, have a system for accessing your passwords so that you never find yourself thwarted from getting into your accounts.

Don't fall foul of fraud

- Never give out any financial details, unless you have contacted your bank yourself.
- Only buy on secure websites: look out for the padlock symbol in the browser window.
- Make your passwords impossible to guess by combining random numbers and letters and vary them for different accounts.

Everyday money management

Knowing what you have and where, and what you owe, is the foundation you need to establish to be able to manage your money on a daily basis. The next step is to form good basic habits that will allow you to keep track of where your money is going, avoid unnecessary wasted expenditure and set up a saving routine.

Start by putting a date in your diary. Set up a monthly money meeting with yourself in which to go through your bank statements to scrutinize your transactions and to go through any bills. This routine is about picking up mistakes – for example being charged for something twice – and about tracking exactly where your money is going.

Budgets and budgeting

Whatever situation you're in practically and financially, set yourself a budget. The budgeting process involves working out what money you have coming in, what you're spending and what you have left over. Part of the point of setting a budget is to be able to plan well so that you don't spend more than you have. But budgeting is also about breaking down your spending so that you can adjust it to make your money go further.

There are lots of useful apps to help simplify your regular budgeting, once you've got started. But when you're putting your first budget together, all you need is a pen and paper, and your phone or a calculator to add up your numbers.

Working out your expenditure

The first thing you need to do is work out your outgoings. Look back over the last calendar month and work out exactly what you spent. The first place to start is your bank statement, where your regular, as well as the majority of your spending will feature. From rent to bills, list your regular monthly expenses. Next, identify your other areas of expenditure. These will include food shopping, snacks and coffees, travel, going out, leisure/hobby-related expenditure, clothes, toiletries, study or work-related expenditure and holidays. Make sure you have a category for each type of spending, and when you get to the end of your list aim to have categorized as much expenditure as possible, including what you bought with any cash withdrawals. If you are using a credit card and making monthly payments, work out exactly what you are buying with the credit card and add the details into your relevant categories.

Working out your income

The next stage in the budgeting process is to work out exactly how much money you have to spend. Once again, look back over the last calendar month and work out how much money you had. When you calculate your available money for that month, include all incoming money, from earnings to student loan payments. You want to set your budget against a typical month's income, so highlight any sources of money you had over that month that were only one-offs, such as birthday money.

Setting yourself a realistic budget

Now you have a breakdown of your expenditure and a breakdown of your income, you can set a realistic budget. A realistic budget will factor in all your necessary expenditure but also give you some room for manoeuvre. As such, rather than budgeting so that your income is exactly the amount you are predicting you will spend, you need to build in a surplus: more money coming in than you plan to have going out. Building some flexibility into your budget is partly to cover unforeseen expenditure and partly to be able to save some money each month. It's likely that in order to achieve a surplus, you will need to find ways to trim your expenditure by buying less and making better and different decisions, so we'll look at how to save money in the next section.

Once you've worked out your overall budget, break it down into categories so that you know how much you have to spend on each part of your life, from groceries to travel. Setting yourself mini budgets in each of your spending categories will help you to stick to your overall budget.

Ultimately budgeting is about lining up your income and expenditure in order to keep track of the exact 'comings and goings' of your money. Budgeting aims not just to stop you running out of money, it's also the only way you can set yourself financial goals, such as saving to have *more* money.

> **TIP:** Automate regular payments where possible. Set up monthly bills as direct debits to avoid paying any late. Late payments can lead to fines as well as negatively impact your credit score.

Saving

The reasons we want to save vary, from having enough money to cover future outgoings to wanting to build up savings for a particular purchase, or as a financial 'cushion'. How we can save also varies, from spending less by buying less, to finding cheaper ways to buy things and dodging expenditure traps. A useful way to think about saving is to split it into two categories: (1) avoiding wasting money: by making smarter spending decisions and getting more disciplined in your buying; and (2) building a savings pot by regularly setting money aside.

Cutting waste

Earlier we talked about making sure you're never wrongly charged for something, which is one way to make sure you don't waste money. Here are some other examples of strategies you can put into practice to help ensure you spend your money wisely:

- Test bigger purchases before you buy them: whether it's a gym membership or a gadget, don't buy it unless you've tried it and know that you will use it.

- Other than food/drink items, only buy things that you can return and get your money back on: there will be times when you change your mind or find a better price elsewhere.

- Don't use cash machines that charge a fee: as a principle, you should *never* be willing to pay to access your own money.

- Buy travel tickets as far in advance as possible to avoid higher prices.

- Get any money back that you're entitled to: always claim for eligible travel delays and get a refund on faulty goods.

- Review any subscriptions you have: how much do you make use of them? Cancel any you aren't getting your money's worth from.

> **TIP:** *Always get and keep a receipt, paper or electronic, and keep them for a month. You'll need one to check that you paid the correct amount, and you don't want to get stuck with something you can't return when you want to.*

Making savings by shopping smarter

As well as cutting waste, you can improve your finances by finding cheaper ways of doing things. Here are just some examples of ways to make small savings that can really add up:

- Find the cheapest, not nearest, supermarket and buy own-brand items; it can also be cost-effective to buy in bulk (eg a bigger pack or multi-pack). Even factoring in a delivery charge you can make savings by using cheaper stores, so ordering online may be the most economical option.

- Use your discounts: sign up for loyalty cards that will save you money and any money-off passes you are eligible for.

- Negotiate where possible: businesses are keen to retain customers, so when it comes to renewing your phone contract, for example, see if you can get them to give you a better deal.

- Don't buy your take-away lunch at sandwich shops: you don't even need to make your lunch at home, simply buying it from a supermarket is much cheaper.

- Don't buy bottled water: get a reusable bottle and keep it filled with tap water.

Setting yourself a savings rate

Alongside cutting your expenditure, you need to get into the habit of saving by regularly putting money aside. Building a savings pot is not only for people with money to spare. However stretched you might feel, you want to get into the habit of saving every month. Regular saving, and establishing a mindset that (whatever financial situation you are in) saving is a priority, are vital. Saving isn't just about building up a fund, it's also part of ensuring you live within your means. The optimal way to save is to set a routine where your saving is automatic, rather than hinging on how the month's spending has gone.

Start by calculating a savings rate. How much can you afford to save each month? Be realistic, but equally set yourself as high a savings goal as possible. Next, identify which savings account will give you the best interest rate. Use one of the many easy-to-understand money comparison websites to identify what would work best for you. Once you've opened a savings account or worked out that an account you already have will give you the best return, set up a monthly direct debit to come out of your current account. Treat your savings sum as a monthly outgoing in your budget, rather than money you 'have' at the end of the month.

Once you've set yourself a regular savings rate, draw up a future savings goal by setting a date for when you would like to up the amount you save each month. Don't plan your goal around a change in your income ie when you have more money, plan it around the idea that the savings you make by spending more efficiently will allow you to put a bit more away. Again, be realistic, so consider raising your savings rate by up to 10 per cent, rather than say, 50 per cent. By setting savings goals, you'll not only be saving more money, you'll be incentivizing yourself to implement cost-cutting measures.

Borrowing

Most of us, at one time or another, will need to borrow money. Whether it is borrowing to pay for our studies or to get a mortgage, loans can enable us to do things we wouldn't otherwise be able to and improve our opportunities. On the flip side, debt can make for a life with severely narrowed options and constant money worries.

Before we go any further, a note on student finance. Many students in England today take out a tuition fee loan to cover course fees, and many also take out a maintenance loan to cover living costs. This chapter refers to borrowing from banks and bank loans, rather than these government-backed student financing arrangements with very different repayment terms. It's nevertheless vital to be familiar with the terms and conditions of any government-backed loans you have.

To be able to borrow well – where the debt you take on is worth it, the risk is calculated and the repayments are manageable – your decisions need to be well informed and very carefully thought out. Whether you are considering buying something on a credit card, or you are applying for a bank loan, the questions you need to ask are:

1 Why do I need to take on debt to do or buy this, are there no alternatives?

2 Do I really need to do or buy this at all?

3 How much more will I end up paying overall, and how will I repay this?

The use of the word 'debt' here, rather than credit or loan, is deliberate. Seeing it as debt rather than describing it more euphemistically is really important. You need to be very clear that you are spending money that you don't have.

As well as making careful decisions about any money you borrow, it's essential that you are fully informed about the exact terms and conditions of any debt/loan, not least because breaching them can be particularly punishing. Looking at the three most common forms of borrowing, make sure that you are clear on the following:

- Credit cards: the minimum monthly payment and the interest rate and whether it will change.

- Loans: the repayment conditions, the repayment schedule and the interest rate.

- Bank overdrafts: how much you are authorized to use, for how long and the interest rate.

What I found useful:

'Live by the rule that if you can't afford something don't buy it. It's really tempting to buy things or do things beyond your means, but when it comes to paying back that extravagant holiday, you'll likely regret it.'

What I wish I'd known:

'That you can resist impulse buys by waiting a day or two. I was amazed by how often the urge to have something waned when I made myself postpone purchases that were not absolutely necessary.'

C.D. (Social anthropologist)

Exercise

Think of something that you regularly buy, say weekly, that you think you could do without. It could be anything from a magazine to a snack. Go for two weeks without buying it and see what difference it makes. Do you really miss it? Is the quality of your life much diminished without it? If the answer is no, work out how much you spend on it a month, stop buying it and add the sum onto your monthly savings rate.

Part Four
Applying for a job

14
Creating a winning CV

Your CV is essentially an advertisement for you. It's where you get to showcase your key information – from your education to your interests – and present yourself in the best possible light. Employers will use your CV not only to find out about the qualifications and experience you have but also to gain insight into the type of candidate you are. From how much attention to detail you display, to your engagement with the industry you're applying to, your CV will play a key role in determining whether your application goes on to the next stage.

In this chapter we'll look at how you can optimize your record and achievements by using effective formatting and making smart decisions about what to include, to produce a CV that impresses employers.

What to include in your CV

Our focus in this chapter is on standard electronic CVs, generally sent to employers via email. In some cases, in industries such as film-making and advertising, a video CV can be desirable. However, even where this applies, employers generally also want a standard electronic version. The format of your CV – the order and detail in which you present your information – can also vary considerably. For example, as you get further into your career, some industries have guidelines on what to include in a CV, from technical skills, to lab work, to research reports. Early on in your career, the so-called 'traditional' standard CV is generally regarded as the best bet – and what we'll concentrate on – rather than a specialist one. The most common format for a traditional CV is to present your educational background and work experience, in reverse chronological order, and if you choose to, relevant additional skills, interests and achievements.

> **TIP:** *It's worth highlighting that your CV should be a 'dynamic' document, which you keep updating and, where applicable, tailor for specific applications.*

Let's start by running through the basics of what your CV should cover by dividing it into two main sections: essential components and optional components. The essentials outline the basic information employers need to know about you, regardless of what other details you decide to include in your CV:

- your **personal information,** including your name and contact details;
- your **education and qualifications;**
- your **experience** including paid work, work experience and voluntary work;
- details about your **references:** either the contact details of your referees or a statement such as 'References available on request'.

The optional elements of your CV offer a lot of scope for flexibility. These are the sections in which you have the opportunity to present your additional skills, interests and achievements. How you categorize this type of additional information comes down to what you want to include, as well as personal preference. So, for example, your CV might have one or more, or a variation, of the following sections:

- **Additional skills.** Here you might include languages (if you speak more than one language fluently, you may want to include a separate 'Languages' section), IT competencies and other training you've undertaken, such as a first aid course.
- **Interests or extracurricular activities.** This section could include hobbies or sports team memberships, for example.
- **Achievements.** Here you might bring in an award you have won, or an accomplishment such as a fundraising success.
- **Personal statement.** This is where you have an opportunity to outline what you have to offer and what you are seeking.

When you decide what you want to present and how, remember that the purpose of your CV is to showcase yourself as effectively as possible. Therefore, make sure (a) that you don't undersell yourself by missing out potentially valuable information, but also (b) that you don't put in superfluous details.

Finally, there's the option of including a personal statement at the start of your CV. Later in the chapter we'll look at whether you really need one and how to put together a pithy summary that actually serves your CV.

What your CV looks like

Visually, your aim when setting out your CV should be to make it as easy to read, simple and professionally presented as possible. Keep in mind that employers are trying to quickly extract information from your CV: fussy fonts and multiple colours run the risk of being an unnecessary distraction.

Here are some basic presentation guidelines:

- **Length.** Your CV should be a maximum of two pages long. Sometimes one-page CVs are recommended for recent graduates, but not if this entails making the font and margins tiny. More than two pages is unnecessarily long.
- **Font type and size.** Use a clear font, such as Times New Roman or Calibri, in 10–12 point, and stick to the same font throughout.
- **Bold.** Use bold for section headings.
- **Bullet points.** Use bullet points to clearly delineate listed items under each heading.
- **Margins.** Use standard-sized margins, avoiding making them too wide or too narrow – noticeable margins are a give-away for either trying to cram too much information in or trying to pad out a thin CV.
- **Heading.** Write your name in larger font, not 'CV', at the header of your first page.
- **Photos.** Unless you are applying for a modelling or acting job, don't include a photo.

When it comes to the design details of your CV, there is lots of scope for variation. You'll find many examples of design templates online that can be helpful for inspiration.

What to cover in each section of your CV

Having looked at an outline of what to include in your CV, let's now look at what to cover in each section in more detail.

Personal information

The main point of the personal details you include is for employers to be able to contact you. As such, they should consist of: your full name, your telephone number (preferably your mobile) and your main email address.

Do not include your date of birth, nationality or marital status – not only do you not have to, so it would be a waste of space, but these things are actually illegal for a potential employer to consider when making a hiring decision. Leaving them off will avoid any risk of conscious or unconscious discrimination. It's also not necessary to include a postal address, and it's unusual to include any social media handles. It's increasingly common to include your LinkedIn handle, but only do so if your profile is up-to-date and of the same strong standard as your CV.

Education and qualifications

When it comes to your education and qualifications, the principle to keep in mind is that the more recent the education, the more details are required. Working on the basis that you are about to finish your degree, or have re-cently done so, your education and qualifications section should run along the following lines and order:

- **Degree.** Here you would include the start and end date of your course, your educational institution, your degree subject and the final or predicted grade. You also have the option of including some details on the breakdown of your performance, for example by year and/or by courses/ modules taken.

- **A levels or equivalent.** Include the start and end date of this period of study, the educational institution, and your subjects and grades.

- **GCSE or equivalent.** Include your start and end dates, the educational institution if it differs from where you did your A levels or equivalent, and the grades achieved. In this section you don't need to give a breakdown of your GCSE/equivalent subjects, just the summary; for example, 11 GCSEs: 5 As, 4Bs, 2Cs, but do include English and maths if you have them, as these are often regarded as minimum requirements.

Experience

Having a single 'Experience' section, rather than separate sections for 'Paid work experience', 'Work experience' and 'Volunteering', allows you to bring together all the work you've undertaken into one strong section. This is a particularly useful CV strategy when the work experience you have as you start out in your career is likely to be limited. By combining these three categories you can showcase the breadth of skills acquired, range of responsibilities held and variety of work undertaken. Your experience section is one with particular scope for tailoring. Use it to identify the elements of your experience that demonstrate that you have been honing relevant skills, regardless of the type of work you have been doing, and whether you were paid or not. Where possible, it can be valuable to link these skills to those listed in the job description. Ensure that you make clear whether each role outlined was paid, unpaid work experience or voluntary work.

Stick to the reverse chronological order format for outlining your experience, and aim to emphasize the elements that will be most pertinent to your job applications. So, for example, if you had a part-time job in a café, you might highlight the requirement to work well under pressure during busy periods and your responsibility for cashing up. When discussing unpaid work experience you have gained in your targeted industry, you should highlight any exposure to specific elements relevant to the job you are applying for. If you have voluntary work experience, note any transferable skills developed, such as organizational skills, alongside your time commitment.

References

The strength of your references lies in good planning: first in choosing the most suitable referees and then in preparing them with the necessary information. For graduate CVs, two referees is standard practice, often consisting of one academic referee and one work-experience-related referee. In both cases, you should choose referees who know you well enough to comment on your work and with whom you have a positive relationship. How and when you ask for a reference is key. Once you have identified a potential referee, write to them to ask whether they would be willing to provide you with a reference. In your request, outline what you are hoping to do next and why (this provides them with the information they need to write you a thorough reference and makes the job easier for them). Only once your potential referee has agreed – *not* before – should you put them down on your CV, if you choose to name your referees. It's also important to give your referees some idea of your application timeframe so that they know broadly when they might be asked to submit a reference. If your referees are called upon by an employer, always write to thank them afterwards, regardless of whether your application is successful or not.

You'll need to decide whether to name your referees, or whether to simply put 'References available on request'. One advantage of naming your referees is that it makes it easier for employers to start the reference requesting process when they already have the relevant details. On the other hand, by not naming your referees, you can be sure that they won't be contacted without your knowledge. Another potential advantage of stating 'References available on request' is that it means you can change your referees if necessary, for example if a referee is unavailable at the point the employer requests your references. If you do name your referees, include their title and role, as well as their role in relation to you (for example, course tutor, line manager), and their contact details (email address and telephone number). If you don't name your referees, you still need to have lined them up so that they are ready to write you a reference at short notice.

Optional CV sections

Additional skills

A useful way to approach an additional skills section is to present an informative list of any potentially relevant skills. We mentioned some suggestions earlier, from languages to first aid skills, and other examples might include IT competencies such as coding. Ideally, the skills you include should be ones that could relate to your professional life. Make sure you include the necessary details for each skill: if you mention languages, for example, put in your competency level.

Interests and achievements

Whether you include additional categories such as 'Interests and achievements', 'Interests' or 'Extracurricular activities' should be determined by the value of what you have to put in them. Accomplishments, from winning an award to getting a distinction in Grade 8 cello, can certainly be worth highlighting. It can also be valuable to draw attention to activities you spend a lot of time on and are genuinely passionate about, be it music or mountain climbing. Don't, however, just include interests for the sake of it, or mundane pastimes such as watching TV or eating out.

Never lie

Many a survey has been released revealing the high proportion of people who 'embroider the truth' in their CVs. Never let this lull you into thinking it's acceptable, and be crystal clear about the dividing line between making the best of your skills and experience, and being dishonest. Even seemingly minor embellishments are ill advised: whether it's the computer programme you've never actually used or the job title you never actually had, they will likely come back to haunt you. A good test is whether you would be embarrassed for anyone to read your CV because of the way you have presented something – if you would be, change it.

Personal statements

Having a personal statement at the beginning of your CV is a matter of choice. The jury is out on them, with some employers keen on a pithy personal summary and others less so. If you do opt for one, it must be informative and short. A bad personal statement runs the risk of putting employers off before they've even looked at your CV properly. For example, it is simply not useful for an employer to read that you think you are an excellent, self-starting candidate with enormous potential – they can make that judgement for themselves.

The best way to approach your decision about whether to use a personal statement is to work out whether it's going to add anything informative to your CV that cannot be covered elsewhere. If, for example, you are targeting a specific role in an industry, a personal statement can be used to highlight your sharp focus. It's also worth finding out what the norm in your industry of choice is, which you can do by looking at guidance on industry-specific CV formats. Personal statements can also be very useful for highlighting important information for employers that doesn't feature elsewhere, for example if you are a non-UK national but have the right to work in the UK.

The big proof

The single most important thing you can do to strengthen your CV is the easiest: ensuring that you don't have any typos or grammatical mistakes in it.

You might have the most impressive record on every count yet find yourself deemed sloppy because you've not spotted a mistake in your CV. Employers take a dim view on the matter: 'It annoys me to see that someone hasn't bothered to proofread their CV: not only does it mean they lack professional judgement by not understanding that errors matter, they are being inconsiderate by making employers wade through shoddy work,' complains a property developer.

Once you have the final draft of your CV for a specific job application, start a thorough proofing process:

- Print your CV out and proofread it very carefully. Look out for formatting issues as well as typos, and pay special attention to incorrect spellings such as stationary (still), when you mean stationery (pens and pencils).
- Enlist a fresh pair of eyes to proofread your amended copy, again printed out.
- Once you have corrected any errors, do a final proofread, on paper and on screen.

As most of your CV will not be in full sentences, typos and spelling mistakes are likely to be your most common source of errors. If you do put in a personal statement, however, make sure your grammar is correct. Don't be tempted to find a short cut to the proofing process using automated spellcheckers: not all errors will be picked up and new ones can creep in as the spellchecker can change the meaning of the word where there are spelling variations.

Your CV as a work in progress

How easy your CV is to read and how well you present your qualifications and experience, are crucial. But it's also worth remembering that the more experience you have and the more achievements you get under your belt, the more potential there is to enhance your CV. You therefore need to think of your CV as an ongoing work in progress that is regularly improved and adapted. As well as including new developments, you also need to update your essential information, from new telephone numbers to your latest grades and, where possible, tailor your CV to reflect particular job specifications. Always reproof your CV and check that the formatting hasn't been affected when you make any changes.

What I found useful:

'I asked a few close friends to send me their CVs so that I could see lots of different formats/approaches (and steal the best ideas!). It was really useful to see a variety of examples to judge the best format, structure and phrases.'

What I wish I'd known:

'I wish I'd known that a very clear and concise CV is more effective than a CV that scrupulously lists every skill and piece of experience I have gained. For example, you can use short bullet points to summarize key responsibilities in past jobs. You can also summarize your education history, rather than listing every exam result. It can be hard to decide to leave out some things, but you can always use your covering letter or application to expand on any detail.'

C.D. (Editor)

Exercise

To help you get into eagle-eyed proofing mode, below are some sentences containing commonly confused spellings. Correct the sentences where the wrong spelling has been used:

1 Tom's company gives out complementary stationery.

2 He has worked their for several years, sourcing led for the company pencils.

3 Tom needs to altar one of his regular orders, because the price of led has become to expensive.

4 He is, however, loathe to change supplier so has prepared a draught offer that he hopes will be excepted.

15
Covering letters and application forms

We've looked at how to put your best self forward in your CV, so in this chapter we'll look at the function that covering letters and applications perform.

In short, both covering letters and application forms are targeted pitches for a specific role at a particular organization. They both also test a range of qualities, from your communication and research skills to the depth of your industry knowledge. Application forms usually include some closed-ended questions that specify the details they require, and key to success is evidencing your answers with concrete examples. They usually also include some open-ended questions that allow more scope for creativity when you are deciding what information to give. Strong answers to these open-ended questions mirror what a well-structured covering letter would include. Over this chapter, therefore, we'll look at how to put together a powerful covering letter and which guidelines to apply to answering application forms.

The purpose of a covering letter

Let's start by looking at what employers are trying to get out of covering letters. The principal question an employer is trying to answer from your covering letter is whether they should take your application to the next stage. To do this, they are seeking to answer a number of subsidiary questions:

- Whether you have the necessary education, skills and experience for the role.
- How you perform in the task of matching your skills and experience to a particular role; including how well you articulate your ideas, and your ability to engage and persuade the employer.

- How you communicate, and specifically how you write; including how clearly you express yourself and your writing skills, from sentence structure to grammar.

- Your professionalism: from whether you correctly address and sign off your letter to whether your letter is well-formatted.

- Your research skills: whether you have found out job, organization and industry information that is pertinent to your covering letter.

- How well you follow instructions: if the application guidelines asked for any specific questions to be addressed, evidence that you have done so.

- Whether you are motivated and enthusiastic about the role.

- Your attention to detail: from identifying the correct person to write to, to ensuring there are no typos.

As one employer (a campaign group director) emphasizes, how good a covering letter is really does matter: 'A large number of our candidates, if not actually the majority, have top grades at A level and good degrees from good universities: covering letters are essential to help us to identify who the stronger candidates are.'

Common covering letter mistakes

A strong covering letter will present a clear outline of why your skills and experience are suited to the job in question and how you would be an asset to the team/department and the wider organization. Arguably the most common mistake applicants make when writing covering letters is to focus on their own CV, making little or no reference to the job and organization they are applying for. The one rule you need to remember for covering letters is that they *must* be tailored to the specific role you are applying for. The employer often already has your CV; the purpose of a covering letter is to demonstrate how what's in your CV fits the job description, not to regurgitate it. A useful practical pointer is to aim for a more or less equal balance between how much you write about yourself and how much you write about the job, organization and industry you're targeting.

Employers will immediately pick up on a 'generic' covering letter in which what amounts to little more than a CV in full prose is being used to apply for multiple jobs. A covering letter that is tailored only by tweaking the name of the employer (and sometimes even this has been known to have been forgotten!) shouts loudly that you haven't given any thought to the particular job you are applying for. As well as revealing that you've put little effort into your letter, this also implies that you're not really that interested in the job or the organization. It's also worth being mindful about the file name you give your letter: avoid labelling it along the lines of 'Version 1 covering letter', for example, which sounds generic, and instead label it '[Full name] covering/cover letter'.

Here are some other commonly made covering letter mistakes that employers complain about:

- **Presumptuousness.** Don't write 'I look forward to discussing my application with you', or similar, as this clearly assumes that you will be invited for interview.

- **Pompousness.** Avoid grand statements such as 'I am certain that I would be an enormous asset to the organization'. Not only does this sound arrogant, there is no information of value to employers in sweeping, unsubstantiated claims.

- **Missing the point of a covering letter.** A classic, and surprisingly common, example of this are covering letters that say little or no more than 'Please find my CV attached', with no reference to skills and experience, the job or organization.

- **Carelessness.** Spelling a name or part of the address wrong, for example.

- **Lack of evidence.** Failing to back up claims. It's not enough to say you are very passionate about something: how can you illustrate this?

Constructing a strong covering letter

Having discussed the purpose of a covering letter and key mistakes to avoid, let's now go through what you need to include in your letter and how to structure it.

The simplest way to break down the writing process is to follow a standard format of questions to answer, within each paragraph, for every covering letter you write. The likelihood is that you will be writing a number of covering letters to different organizations, and the more systematic your approach to writing them, the more manageable the task. Splitting your letter into sections makes it both easier to write and gives you a checklist to work from so you don't miss anything out. Do also keep in mind that some employers will ask you to address specific questions in your covering letter: ensure you fully address what they have asked you to do.

What to cover in each paragraph of a covering letter

Paragraph 1: Factual introduction

Set out the purpose of your letter and your basic profile as an applicant in the opening paragraph. This first section should be short, sticking to only essential facts.

Key information:

- The job you are applying for, including the full title of the role and the name of the organization.
- Where you saw the job advertised or how you heard about it.
- Your current status, eg final year [subject] undergraduate at [name of university/college].

Paragraph 2: Your expression of interest

Your pitch for the job starts here, so this paragraph needs to be punchy and persuasive. The purpose of this part of your letter is to prove your enthusiasm and suitability for the job, by demonstrating how well you understand the role and how well acquainted you are with the organization and the wider industry. It is also where you have the opportunity to provide some insight into how you would approach the job.

Don't simply rehash the job description in this section; instead, using your background research, explain how the job will help you to achieve your goals, what appeals to you about the organization and what makes the opportunity one you have been looking for. You can introduce (but not yet go into detail on) your own skills, experience and interests in this paragraph by giving examples of how the job would draw on and help you to develop these. This section is not just about what you will get out of the role but, crucially, why you want it. This paragraph, along with paragraph 3, below, should make up the bulk of your covering letter.

Key information:

- Why you want the job.
- Why you would like to work for the organization.
- Why you want to work in the sector.

Paragraph 3: Your suitability for the role

This is the point in your covering letter where you illustrate to the employer how your specific skills and experience will enable you to do the job well. Each time you refer to having a skill or relevant experience, you need to include concrete evidence. This section provides you with the chance to elaborate on achievements you are only able to touch on in your CV. It's also worth emphasizing that rather than just matching the required competencies to your own, your aim should be to demonstrate why you would *excel* in the role. To give an example, rather than simply saying you have suitable research experience, you could highlight the top mark you achieved in your final year dissertation, giving details of how your approach to the research contributed to this.

Key information:

- The skills you have that relate to the required competencies for the job.
- The relevant experience you have.
- A summary of the contribution you can make to the organization.

Paragraph 4: Final word

This last part of the letter needs to be no longer than a line but is invaluable for leaving a positive, polite and professional impression. Courtesy goes a long way in applications, particularly when employers are used to having to trawl through a large number of careless covering letters. So, thank the employer for considering your application.

Covering letters for speculative applications

The main difference when you are writing a covering letter for a speculative application is that it's up to you to identify the type of work you are looking for and where you could fit into the organization. The key is to work out how your skills and experience could benefit the organization, by carefully researching its priorities and identifying a gap you could fill.

Presentation and formatting

Having thought about what to include in your covering letter, you now need to think about how much space you will have overall so that you can work out roughly how long each paragraph should be, as well as paying attention to the clarity and professionalism of your presentation.

- The standard length is no longer than one side of A4.
- Half a page is probably too short.

- Standard sized margins, as with your CV.
- Use one clear font in 10–12 point size.
- Your address goes on the right-hand side at the top.
- The recipient's name/address goes on the left-hand side just below that.
- The date of the letter goes on the right-hand side just above the body of the letter.

Addressing your covering letter

Who you address your covering letter to will depend on the information you have. Make every effort to ensure that you follow any instructions you are given on who to apply to: if the application process states who you should address applications to, failing to do so does not stand you in good stead. If you are given a name, make sure you spell it correctly, and ensure you get their title right. Identify titles that are not stated by looking the person up on the organization's website or LinkedIn. If a particular title such as 'Dr' isn't stated, use Ms for female and Mr for male employers. It is becoming increasingly common for first names to be used to address covering letters; however, erring on the side of formality remains the safest option. If no name is given, address your covering letter to 'Sir or Madam' (note that there is no 'e' at the end in the UK spelling). Both named and unnamed addresses should be preceded by 'Dear', with 'Yours sincerely' used to end the letter when the person you are writing to is named, and 'Yours faithfully' when your covering letter is addressed to 'Sir or Madam'. Finally, end your letter by typing out your full name – there's no need to insert a signature.

Emailing your covering letter

Covering letters are most commonly requested electronically and rarely by post. A good way to email your covering letter is to attach it to an email as a Word document or PDF, along with your CV (if applicable). In the body of the email, address the employer as you do in your covering letter, and write a note to say that you are applying for job x and that your covering letter and CV (if it has been requested) are attached. The subject of the email should be along the lines of 'Application for [job title]' including a job reference number where applicable.

Proofing

Finally, a proofing process for your covering letter is essential. Start by going through each name to ensure you have the correct spelling, and then do a thorough proof of your letter as a whole, working from a printout. Look out for common covering letter errors: the wrong spelling of a word in the given context, missing articles (eg a, the), repeated words (eg 'that that') and rogue or forgotten apostrophes.

Application forms

Application form questions can range from basic factual questions, to questions looking for much more detailed responses. For questions requiring extended answers, as we noted earlier, the overlap with covering letters is considerable. For example, application forms often ask for a statement outlining your interest in a role. This open-ended question can be approached by following the guidelines that we looked at for the corresponding section of a covering letter.

Here are a few basic principles to apply more generally when you're filling in an application form:

- Follow instructions for each question very carefully: look out for specific details required in your answers.

- Wherever possible, eg when referring to your skills and experience, back your answers up with specific examples. You may find it helpful to use the 'STAR' method to structure your examples (see Chapter 16 for more on the technique).

- Never leave a question unanswered: if you are a suitable candidate, there won't be a single question on which you don't have something to say. If, for example, you do not have a particular skill, outline how you are addressing this.

- Where applicable, be guided by the amount of space you've been given: you shouldn't find yourself with a lot of space left, neither should you struggle to fit in your answer.

- On a practical level, make sure you are saving your answers as you complete the form. It's all too easy to lose what you've done so far when filling in an online form. It's also worth saving a copy of your answers for online application forms, so that you can re-read your answers before any interviews.

TIP: *It's often said that you shouldn't refer to skills or experience in your covering letter or application form that are not on your CV. One way to approach this advice is to decide that if it's relevant in your covering letter/ application form, it would likely also be an asset on your CV.*

Deadlines

Writing good covering letters and filling in applications well requires planning, which requires time. Before you start to even think about what you are going to write, make sure you know when the exact deadline is. There is frequently confusion about the meaning of closing dates. For example, if the closing date is 15 June, should the application be in *before* the 15th or can it be in *on* the 15th? The general rule is that the closing date is inclusive, meaning it is the final day on which your application will be accepted. To be on the safe side, get your application in by the end of the working day, 5pm, on the closing date. With the deadline in mind, work out how long you have to submit your application and then divide your time up into research and preparation, writing, editing and proofing.

What I found useful:

'One of the most useful things I ever did was to start thinking about my work experience not in terms of qualifications or actual tasks (ie not what I did on a day-to-day basis) but thinking more holistically about my skill set ie what those day-to-day tasks amount to put together, or the "essence" of those tasks, to put it another way. I found this approach particularly helpful when looking for opportunities that weren't directly in my field of expertise but where I could show through my applications/covering letters that I had relevant experience and was therefore worth considering as a candidate.'

What I wish I'd known:

'I've come to see that you need to think more creatively and less literally about how you present yourself to employers. Being able to sell oneself is a skill that successful people are adept at. This doesn't mean stretching the truth about what you've done or the skills you have; it means understanding what employers want and shaping what you have to offer accordingly.'

V.L. (Business development manager)

Exercise

Go back to an application form you completed in the past and still have a copy of. It can be an application for a job or for education (for example your UCAS application). Go through the application and identify whether you think there are any weaknesses in it. Thinking back to the tips we've looked at on covering letters and application forms, as well as the mistakes employers complain about, is there anything you would now do differently?

16
Interviews

Being invited to an interview marks the clearing of a key hurdle: you've shown the employer that it's worth taking your application to the next stage. Now you need to convince the employer that you would be the *best* candidate – that your skills and experience are the most suitable for the job, that you would make the most out of the opportunity and that you have the greatest potential.

Interviews are often the part of the job application process that makes candidates most nervous, largely because they are 'live'. Bear in mind, however, that employers are not trying to catch you out when they interview you, and interview nerves are not something that would put them off. The employer's aim is to work out whether you would be an asset to their organization. How well prepared you are, on the other hand, can make a big difference to how well you do in the interview. So, in this chapter, we'll look at how to ensure you are equipped to do your best: from what to find out before the interview, to how to tackle questions during it.

Types of interviews

We'll focus on standard interviews in this chapter, where a single candidate is interviewed. We'll touch on other formats, such as group interviews, when we discuss assessment centres in the next chapter.

Standard interviews are based on a question and answer model, but can differ in their focus and form. The number of interviewers might vary from one to a panel of several people, and not all interviews happen face-to-face. Telephone/Skype interviews are now common, and video interviews are used increasingly, particularly for first interviews when the selection process involves more than one stage. As well as the number of interviews, the type of questions can also vary, with some interviews focusing on competencies, others on strengths, and many bringing in a combination of competency-based and strength-based questions. Another element of variability is whether the interview is accompanied by a psychometric or technical skills test (also discussed in the next chapter). The level of formality can also differ considerably between interviews, from those that are more scripted and based around a set of specific questions, to interviews that feel more like an informal conversation.

Preparing for an interview

Once you've been invited for an interview, make sure you find out everything you can about what it will involve. The employer will give you as much or as little detail as they want, and this may include who is interviewing you. It is more common for employers to inform you about who will be conducting the interview than not, so when you're given this information make sure you do some background research on them. Look them up on the organization's website and identify their particular responsibilities and expertise, as well as finding out what they've been working on recently, where possible. It's always worth asking employers whether you should prepare anything in particular for the interview. A good opportunity to do this is when you accept an interview invitation: while most employers will not require specific preparation, enquiring can sometimes elicit useful insight into the interview focus, for example if the employer suggests reading up on a particular project. Some larger (often global) organizations are widely known to use a set style for interviews. Larger organizations also often provide details of how they assess candidates, with examples of skills and competencies they are looking for, so it's always worth scrutinizing the 'Careers'/ 'Jobs'/ 'Work for us' section of an organization's website.

Start your pre-interview preparation by making sure you are wholly familiar with:

- the job description;
- the organization;
- the wider industry (refer back to Chapter 8 on getting up to speed with the latest developments and news).

Having done your background research on the role, organization and industry, the next step in your preparation is to think about the questions you might be asked.

> **TIP:** *Find out whether your university/college careers service offers mock interviews. Many institutions do, and it's an invaluable way to road test how well prepared you are, as well as hone your interview technique.*

Interview questions

Any interviews you have will be based around answering questions. As mentioned earlier, the nature of the questions will vary, with some focusing on competencies, some aiming to identify your strengths, and less structured interviews often including a combination of question types that aim to identify both your skills and strengths. Competency-based questions primarily aim to test whether you have specific skills related to the job you are applying for and frequently start with 'Give an example of...' or 'Describe a situation when...'. Strength-based questions are based on positive psychology and often include questions that focus on your preferences and motivations.

Common questions

Although the specific questions you'll be asked in an interview will differ considerably, variations of certain key questions frequently come up. Let's look at some of the more common questions and what you should consider in your answers.

- **Give an example of when you had to solve a problem.** A good approach to take to these types of behavioural questions is the 'STAR' method. Structure your answers by describing the Situation (the background, for example, where you were working and your role), the Task (or Target: what you were trying to achieve), the Action (what you did to fulfil the task) and the Result (the outcome). The problem itself doesn't need to be dramatic; rather, your aim should be to discuss a problem you solved that allows you to showcase a number of skills.

- **What are your strengths and weaknesses?** Pick a strength that allows you to demonstrate your passion and enthusiasm, and something you are proud of, rather than one you think will impress the employer. Pick a weakness that really is a weakness – answers along the lines of 'I work too hard' or 'I'm a perfectionist' just sound artificial and weak. It will be a strength in itself if you are able to show that you recognize your weaknesses and can implement plans to address them.

- **Where do you see yourself in five years?** Here you can outline what you would like to achieve career-wise and an overview of your step-by-step plan for doing so. Focus your response on how you plan to develop within the industry you are applying to. It can also be helpful to link your answer to your hope that you will get the job you are being interviewed for.

- **Where else have you applied to?** If you haven't applied to other organizations, name ones you are interested in applying to and why. As well as showing employers that you have contingency plans, this gives you the opportunity to demonstrate your industry knowledge.

- **Why did you choose your studies?** Your aim here should be to link the relevance of your studies to the role you are applying for and how the skills you developed will help you to succeed in it. In some cases, the specific subject matter of your degree may be more difficult to directly apply, so focus on drawing out relevant transferable skills.

- **Why do you want to work here?** This is your opportunity to discuss your understanding of the organization, as well as the wider industry, linking your competencies to its needs.

It's worth keeping in mind that employers are generally more interested in how you think, communicate and reason in your answers, than they are in getting one particular response. In other words, the aim isn't to get the *right* answer, but rather to give strong answers that showcase what you have to offer.

You won't be able to foresee all the questions that you'll be asked, so a good strategy is to work out what you would want to cover in your answers, across a range of themes:

- your career goals;
- your experience;
- your education;
- your particular interest in the role;
- your view on what is unique about the organization.

When working out what to include in your answers, as well as bringing in your knowledge about the job (from your earlier preparation to understand the job description and organization), you should re-familiarize yourself with your CV and what you wrote in your covering letter and/or application form. It's surprisingly easy to forget what you wrote down, and it's vital that you can recall your application in your interview, so that an employer's reference to a skill, experience or specific answer doesn't throw you. As you prepare your answers to common questions, try to predict any weaknesses the employer might raise following your answer. For example, if you lack a particular skill, make sure you have an action plan you can tell them about ie how you plan to gain this skill

Some basic rules for good answers

Whatever question you are asked, apply these basic principles when answering:

- As with your written application, always tailor your answers to the specific job and organization.
- Listen carefully to every question that you are asked, and make sure you directly answer each one.
- Even where you haven't been asked for one, give an example in your answer.
- Elaborate on details in your answer.
- Be honest if you don't know the answer to a question, or if you don't have the competency they ask about. As well as accompanying honesty with an outline of your plans to remedy any weaknesses, don't be afraid to show initiative by having a stab at trying to work out an answer that you don't already know.
- Be clear. If you find yourself getting stuck in a rambling answer, reiterate your main point in one short sentence and stop talking.

Any questions?

A question that is asked at the end of virtually every interview is whether *you* have any questions. While one of the purposes of this question is to clarify any uncertainties, what you ask can also yield additional information for the employer. Not having any questions to ask won't necessarily disadvantage you – although it is worth noting that some employers believe that it can be taken as a negative. Asking a weak question, however, won't do you any favours, while asking an excellent question can work in your favour. A classic example of a bad question is one that was answered in the interview or application instructions. The employer will think you haven't been listening or that your attention to detail is lacking.

Examples of good questions:

- Practical ones, such as what happens next in the application process and where you would be based.
- Questions that demonstrate your interest in and understanding of the organization, industry and role, such as future expansion plans and what a typical day might entail.

As well as questions that have already been answered, here are some other pitfalls to avoid:

- Asking for basic information that you would be expected to already know from your own preparation.
- Questions that suggest you've misunderstood the role.
- Inappropriate questions where you start interviewing the interviewer, such as 'What career goals are you hoping to achieve?' This is a surprisingly common mistake: candidates are trying to show interest and confidence but can come across as unprofessional.

Discussing money

Although salary doesn't always come up in interviews, go into each one prepared with a clear idea of your salary expectations to avoid being caught off guard.

Practical planning

Making sure you have all the necessary practicalities in order is essential to ensuring that things don't go wrong on the day. While you're busy preparing, it's easy to make a mistake such as realizing at the last minute that you don't know the exact location for the interview; or that your only smart trousers are still at the dry cleaners. Run through this checklist on the day before your interview (at the very latest):

- Make sure you know the exact address of where you are going, and put it into your phone or print a map.

- Plan your route to the interview, allowing at least an extra 45 minutes for travel disruptions.

- Plan and lay out your outfit, from ties to tights, to avoid any on-the-morning crises or hunts. Always opt for a smart outfit, but also make sure you're comfortable. It can be very distracting for both you and the interviewer if you're shifting around in something uncomfortable or if you're worried that something is going to come undone or ride up.

- Keep up with what's going on in the news, inside the industry and in the wider world. Questions relating to topical issues may arise in the interview, and/or current affairs may crop up in small talk before and after.

On the day

The single biggest mistake you can make at an interview is to be late, so make sure you arrive on time. Keep in mind that being punctual does *not* mean arriving for the interview very early – employers don't want candidates to turn up 45 minutes before the interview, if that's not what they were asked to do. A good trick is to find the exact location of your interview and then walk around the block or have a coffee nearby. Make your way back so that you arrive no more than five minutes early for the interview. Just before you walk into the building switch off your phone (keep it on until then, in case the employer needs to get hold of you/you need to get hold of the employer). It's also worth bringing a small bottle of water with you, in case your throat goes dry during the interview and water isn't provided.

> **TIP:** *Skip the pungent aftershave/perfume on the day of your interview. Employers have been known to speed up interviews when a candidate's cologne has been too intense to bear for long, and even at best it can be an unhelpful distraction.*

The interview itself

One of the mistakes interviewees can make on the day is to focus too much on trying to give their prepared answers, at the expense of fully engaging with the interviewer(s). Here are some basic tips to follow:

- Listen: really pay attention to what is being said rather than just waiting for your turn to speak.

- Avoid interrupting.

- Make direct eye contact, but don't overdo it to the point of staring.

- Keep your body language open and friendly.

- Smile and try to actually enjoy what will generally be a stimulating conversation.

- Don't speak too quickly: be aware that you are likely to speak faster when you are nervous.

- Watch out for so-called 'fillers', such as repeatedly saying the word 'like' or the phrases 'you know' and 'to be honest'.

- Concentrate and maintain a professional manner until the very end of the interview (that is, until you've left the building) so that you give a good final impression.

Tips for video interviews

- Ensure you have a quiet space for the interview, where you won't be interrupted.

- Set up your computer in advance, and make sure everything is working, from the audio to the webcam.

- Make sure your internet connection is good.

- Ensure that you aren't going to be distracted by emails, instant messaging and any other notifications popping up on your computer during the interview.

- Dress smartly.

- Check that there aren't any visual 'distractions' in your background such as an unmade bed.

- Turn your phone off.

- Behave as you would in a face-to-face interview, from eye contact to body language.

After the interview

Tempting as it may be to write and thank the interviewer for seeing you, especially if it went well, it's generally not welcomed. It can be seen as inappropriate, fills up the employer's inbox unnecessarily and risks looking as though you are trying to curry favour. Instead, do as instructed. In the comparative calm of your journey back from the interview, run through any instructions you were given in the interview and jot them down. For example, were you asked to send anything, such as a work sample? Were any referee contact details asked for? Also write down any timeframes that were given, for example when you would be informed as to whether you were shortlisted.

What happens next?

If your interview went well, you may be asked to attend another interview, to complete a further task, or you may be offered the job. (See Chapter 19 for what to do if you are offered a job.) If the employer informs you that your application was unsuccessful, always write back to thank them. As well as being a basic courtesy and professional, it's an opportunity to ask for feedback. Ensure you are specific in your feedback request, for example enquiring about any skills they recommend you develop or experience they think you would benefit from.

Finally, remember to treat interviews as learning experiences. Take on board feedback you get from employers, and work out what you think could have gone better in the interview and what you could improve about your interview technique.

What I found useful:

'When preparing for an interview, I've learned to take a bit of time to think about experiences I've had that can help illustrate my answers. For instance, when things went wrong and I had to come up with a solution quickly, so that when the interviewer asks, I'm not trying to think of an example on the spot. Sure, I won't know the exact questions the interviewer is asking, but having a couple of stories in mind means I'm not flustered trying to think of a good example under pressure in the moment.'

What I wish I'd known:

'Take a look at the company website before the interview. I was pretty embarrassed at the end of an interview when I asked if there were plans to expand into any new locations, and it turned out that they'd recently posted a big announcement about their expansion plans on their website. It was big news at the company, so I felt I looked silly for not knowing about it already!'

A.L. (Business operations manager)

Exercise

Imagine that you have got a job in your target industry and you are now hiring someone to work with you. What would you want to know about them? What questions would you ask them in order to find out about qualities that couldn't be elicited from their CV? How would you try to find out whether you would work well together? Now think about how you would respond to these same questions in an interview.

17
Assessment centres

Sometimes also referred to as a selection centre, an assessment centre is a simulated context in which a mixture of group exercises and individual tasks are used by employers to look at how you would operate in a workplace. The aim of having a number of different types of exercise is to elicit a range of skills, with a view to gaining a more rounded picture of the candidate.

A key difference between assessment centres and other forms of interview is that candidates are tested within a group context. As well as testing a variety of attributes, employers are looking at how candidates interact with others. Typically run over one or two days, assessment centres allow employers to gauge candidates over a longer period than, for example, in an interview. Often used as the final stage of the recruitment process, employers also use assessment centre exercises to observe how well candidates work under pressure.

Assessment centres can also provide *you* with valuable information. As well as being an opportunity to learn more about the organization and role that you are applying for, the exercises you do can provide you with very useful insights into how you work, which skills you have developed and which competencies and qualities need honing or further development.

The specific activities, the format of the assessment day(s) and how tasks are graded will vary across organizations. In this chapter we will therefore look at a general overview of what happens in assessment centres, including the key competencies employers are assessing and examples of the tests they use to do so, general tips on how to prepare for the assessments and advice on how to ensure you do your best on the day(s).

An overview of the assessment process

Let's start by getting an overview of how assessment centres work, from where they are held to who is involved.

Assessment centres are generally used by larger organizations and are often based at their headquarters, although some organizations use hotels and conference centres. Assessments often last a day but can be as short as half a day or as long as a week. Over the course of the assessment process, you will be observed and assessed as you participate in group tasks, as well as on individual tasks. The size of the group you are assessed in will vary, but it's common for there to be around eight people in a group.

The assessors observing you may be assessment specialists with a human resources (HR) background, members of the organization's HR team and/or line managers. Managers or HR staff from the organization you are applying to are more likely to run any interviews, so that they can draw on their knowledge of the role and organization in their questioning. Less commonly, psychologists are also brought in to observe behaviour, and on occasion actors are brought in to perform in role-play scenarios.

As you are being observed the assessors will generally mark you against specific competencies, grading your performance in each exercise, taking notes on how you approach tasks and putting together an assessment of your overall performance.

The first assessment day tends to start with an introduction about the organization you have applied to, sometimes referred to as an 'information session' and often delivered as a presentation. Informal discussion will often then follow, offering candidates the opportunity to ask questions about the organization. An ice-breaker exercise, where, for example, you might be asked to talk briefly about any hobbies, is designed to get candidates 'warmed up' and will frequently precede the start of the day's assessments. The day, or final day if it is over more than one, will often end in a networking or social event. During the day(s) there will generally be one or two coffee breaks, and more often than not lunch will be provided.

The assessments

The point of an assessment centre is to simulate the types of tasks and scenarios that you would experience in the role you are applying for. Ranging from individual timed exercises to practical activities undertaken as a group, you'll be tested through a combination of some of the following assessment methods:

- interviews, including panel interviews with a number of interviewers;
- written exercises including:

o letter drafting;

o case studies;

o 'in-tray' and 'inbox' exercises;

o psychometric tests, including aptitude tests (testing verbal/numerical reasoning) and personality questionnaires. It's worth noting that this type of testing is commonly used as part of the screening for assessment centres;

- group exercises;
- discussions;
- practical tasks;
- social events and networking;
- presentations, both done individually and as a group;
- role playing;
- evaluation/debriefing.

Key to success in an assessment centre context is demonstrating that you have the skills and characteristics the employer is looking for. To do this, you need to understand and familiarize yourself with what each type of task is testing. So, let's now look at which skills and qualities the most common types of assessments are trying to identify. As we go through each assessment method, we'll also look at some pointers for optimizing your performance.

Interviews

Assessment days often include interviews. There may be a single one-to-one interview, or sessions with several interviewers, either in a series of one-to-ones or in the form of an interview panel. Doing well in these draws on the same principles as traditional interviews (see Chapter 16). Run through your job, organization and industry research, your answers for commonly asked questions, and keep in mind the basic principles for good answers.

Written exercises

Case studies

Case studies are essentially problem-solving exercises, where candidates need to digest and interpret information. You are likely to be tested on how you summarize and analyse a problem, the logic and method of your process for solving it, and how clearly and persuasively you justify your decisions. As with most assessments, you need to keep careful track of time, break the task down into steps and communicate your approach as clearly as possible.

Inbox/in-tray exercises

These exercises are aiming to gauge how you organize and prioritize tasks, as well as how you analyse and communicate information. Completing inbox/in-tray tasks well hinges on deciding what must be done and how, quickly; a key test here is how effectively you work under pressure. Identify which messages are most important, focusing on responding to these in the most appropriate way, both in terms of how you communicate (formally/informally) and the decisions you make on what course of action to take, for example, in addressing a complaint.

Psychometric tests

Verbal, numerical and abstract aptitude tests

This type of testing is designed to examine your reasoning and cognitive skills. How you interpret and evaluate data and other forms of information will generally be a focus, as will accuracy on, for example, spelling or mathematical questions. The tests are often based on multiple-choice questions, taken on a computer and in timed conditions. In many cases you will already have taken a similar test online prior to the assessment day, and you'll be repeating the exercise to confirm your results for the employer. Test practice really makes a difference to how well you do in aptitude testing, so aim to get in as much practice as possible. You'll find lots of free psychometric tests to practise with online, and your university/college's careers service will also very likely be able to offer you practice opportunities, as well as test training. Use a variety of tests, especially if you haven't done much maths since school. Tight timings are one of the greatest challenges in aptitude tests, and plenty of practice can help you get quicker at doing them.

Personality questionnaires

These types of tests don't have 'correct' answers and instead seek to understand how you would handle different situations, how you would work with others and in some cases aim to identify your personality 'group'. There isn't a preferred personality type, and it's vital that you answer the questions in a personality questionnaire honestly. Trying to choose answers that you think will be preferable to employers simply risks revealing a disingenuous approach, through an inconsistent set of responses. There's no need to practise personality tests, but it's worth familiarizing yourself with their general format.

Group activities

When you are being assessed as part of a group, the exercises are likely to run along the following lines:

- **Discussions.** These are often based around a case study or involving a problem-solving scenario and generally focused on issues relevant to the organization.
- **Tasks.** Group tasks may centre on a practical activity, for example having to make something working as a team.
- **Role plays.** These would generally be based on a scenario you would experience in the job you are applying for, for example a customer service situation.
- **Social activities.** These might include meals, coffee breaks and networking opportunities.

Group exercises are used to observe how you interact with others but also to scrutinize other qualities more specific to the exercise. So, for example, in a discussion, employers may also be looking at how you absorb information and subsequently summarize it for others. Engaging fully with your group is key, from really listening to other candidates and taking their contributions on board, to helping keep the group focused on the task and communicating your ideas in a persuasive but not domineering manner. Group exercises are an opportunity to deploy the teamwork and, where appropriate, leadership skills, discussed in Chapter 5. The strength of your verbal communication, from expressing your ideas coherently and clearly, to giving constructive feedback, will also help you to perform well.

Always be 'on'

Not all social activities are assessed, but it's best to assume that they are. Social interactions provide a good opportunity to build relationships with other candidates that can be valuable during group exercises. Being open and friendly, and drawing others into the conversation, will help assessors to see your people skills.

Presentations

You might be asked to give a presentation alone or as part of a group, and you may either be asked to prepare it in advance of the assessment day or within a given timeframe on the day. Assessors will be looking at how well prepared your presentation is, how closely you have stuck to the remit of what you were asked to do, and how clearly and confidently you deliver your presentation. In this context, assessors may also see how you handle questions at unexpected points, and possibly also how you deal with last minute changes to the focus of your presentation. We'll look at what makes for successful presentations in the next chapter, but essentials include demonstrating good preparation, coherent and engaging delivery, and sticking to time limits.

Debrief

At the end of the assessment process, candidates will often be asked to reflect on and analyse their performance across the exercises. From an assessment perspective, a central purpose of this part of the day is for employers to see how self-aware you are. Identify exercises where you think your performance could be improved, giving suggestions of what you could have done differently as well as any relevant skills you think could be strengthened and how. The assessors will likely be looking for evidence that you are able to critically assess your own performance, therefore careful reflection and honesty are key. Find concrete examples of what you found difficult and what you enjoyed, and if you were working in a group or observed others, mention elements of their performance that you think were strong. It's also worth preparing thoughts on where you think you will perform less well in the assessments, before the day. If you don't struggle in tasks you'd expected to but do in tasks you thought you'd find easier, for example, bring this information, and some thoughts on why that happened, into the debrief.

Preparing for an assessment centre

However strong a candidate you are, preparation for assessment centre testing is essential. From organizing the necessary practicalities in advance, to doing practice tests, preparation can make a big difference to how you perform.

Study the brief carefully

First make sure that you have read all the information you've been given about the assessment centre. In some cases, employers will ask you to prepare for an exercise on the day, so ensure that you follow any instructions carefully. Employers will generally give you some details on the assessments they will be carrying out and often also what to practise. Keep in mind that this information may be on the organization's website rather than sent to you, so go through all the recruitment process material they have available. It's also worth emphasizing that the skills you will be tested on will generally be outlined in the job description. Employers are not trying to surprise you in what they seek to find, so go through the job advertisement noting the required skills and qualities, and keep them at the forefront of your mind at the assessment centre.

Task and test practice

Even if practice doesn't make your performance perfect, it will mean that you are well prepared. Most of the individual tasks we have looked at can be practised, with practice materials widely available online and through your university or college careers service. Where possible, aim to replicate assessment centre conditions, such as giving yourself limited time in which to complete tasks. Some careers services also offer workshops that run through the types of exercises you'd be assessed on at an assessment centre and even give you one-to-one coaching for them. Make the most of every available practice opportunity, and ask your careers service whether they have feedback from past students about their assessment centre experiences.

Revisiting your application and getting up to speed with the organization and wider industry

As recommended in the last chapter for interview preparation, go through your application materials before attending an assessment centre. From your application form and/or covering letter, to your CV and any interviews you've had, refresh your memory on what you've written, and, if you've had an interview, remind yourself of what it focused on as well as the strengths and weaknesses in your performance. Just as you would for an interview, also ensure that you read up as much as possible about the organization and the wider industry.

Practicalities to prepare

Follow the pre-interview practicalities' drill: prepare your clothes, identify the exact location and plan your journey. If you're staying at a hotel the night before, make sure you know exactly where to go for the first assessment day, and leave enough time in the morning in case you get lost.

On the day

When going into an assessment centre, the right attitude is vital. A common misconception about assessment centres is that you are competing against the other candidates; in reality, however, you are being assessed against the employer's desired competencies, and in some cases all or none of you may be recruited. This more positive approach can make a significant difference: you need to tackle exercises with the aim of being *your* best rather than *the* best, and crucially, cooperating well with others, rather than being competitive, will help you to do that. Along with this mindset, it's also worth following these three basic rules during the assessments:

- **Listen to or read instructions very carefully.** It's easy to panic, not take in instructions fully and find you have misunderstood a task half-way through. Not following instructions properly is one of the most common mistakes candidates make and can slow you down considerably.

- **Time management should be at the forefront of your mind.** A key part of the day's testing will be on your time-management and organizational skills, so work out your timings at the start of each exercise and try to stick to them.

- **Keep moving on.** Approach the assessment day(s) as a whole, rather than focusing on specific tasks: if you struggle in an exercise, tackle the next one without worrying about how you performed in the last. Keep in mind that you won't be good at everything; just as your skills are better in some areas than others, you will do less well in some of the tests. Never fall into the trap of losing motivation if you feel you have performed badly in an activity: carry on positively, aiming to demonstrate your strengths elsewhere.

After the assessment

Having experts carefully scrutinize your competencies provides you, as well as employers, with invaluable information. Therefore, whether you get the job or not, make sure you get as much feedback as possible from the assessments. The assessors' evaluation of your performance across different tasks can amount to very useful advice on areas to develop, as well as providing useful insights into where your strengths currently lie and aspects of your performance that you should aim to replicate. It's also worth reflecting on your own assessment of how you did. Look at whether your performance in each task was scored as you would have expected. Aim to work out what you need to do differently, or what you need to hone if you didn't meet a competency. Did you score less well in an exercise because you didn't get a skill across effectively, and, if so, why was that, or do you need to put more work into developing that skill?

What I found useful:

'I very nearly didn't turn up to the assessment centre. I was sure that I didn't want a corporate job. I looked up the hotel while I was half-heartedly packing to check if I needed a towel. I found out it was a five-star hotel, which I thought sounded fancy, so I went along. It's terrible that my love of luxury towels changed my career. Because I was quite relaxed about the whole thing I was really listening during the assessments. I think sometimes nerves mean you stop engaging and just panic. I asked actual questions – properly challenging questions. I also didn't speak up too often and focused on where I was comfortable. It's easy to become really overbearing in these situations. When I got the call to say I'd got a place I remember being gobsmacked to hear how few of the group had got through. I guess not thinking about competition during the assessments, by not fully appreciating how competitive it was, might also have helped me.'

What I wish I'd known:

'I thought I really wanted to work in start-ups, but I now realize that I'd underestimated how much value there is in really quality training, which I got working in established global companies. The few years I spent in a big consumer goods company really set up my career.'

L.U. (Brand manager)

Exercise

Thinking about the industry you're targeting, sketch out an assessment centre day for a specific job you're interested in applying for. If you were trying to find the most suitable candidate, what skills, personal characteristics and competencies would you be looking to identify? Drawing on the assessment methods discussed in this chapter, how would you test candidates to identify these?

18
Giving presentations

You will very likely need to do presentations during your career, and you may also find yourself being asked to do one to *launch* it – in other words, to do a presentation as part of a job application process.

Presenting is ultimately about informing and engaging your audience. Effective presentations are therefore built through a combination of well-researched and well-organized material, and a delivery that communicates this material clearly and powerfully.

When you are required to do a presentation as part of a job application – what we'll refer to as 'interview presentations' in this chapter – you will have the opportunity to demonstrate a wide range of skills and attributes. From industry knowledge and understanding of the organization's ethos and priorities, to strong research, communication and organizational skills, interview presentations are useful to employers because they provide valuable insight into a candidate's capabilities.

Over this chapter we'll look at what's needed to prepare effective presentations, going through the basics step by step, from identifying the purpose of each presentation to setting yourself up for a smooth delivery.

Your presentation remit

All presentations serve to impart information of some sort to an audience. As a presenter, your aim for what the audience *does* with that information will, however, differ. For example, you may be asked to bring your audience up to speed on a particular subject. Alternatively, your task might be to persuade your audience to buy something, use your services or take on a particular viewpoint. Regardless of your specific remit, an effective presentation will include the same elements: well-targeted research with the presentation's purpose in mind, effectively summarized information, strong delivery and efficient time management.

Over your career, the focus of the presentations you do will differ hugely, as will the audiences you are presenting to. Within the context of a job application, what you are asked to present on will also vary across application processes, as will the time you have to prepare and deliver it. For example, you may be asked to prepare for a presentation at an assessment centre, with advance warning before you attend, or with very little notice as an exercise on the day itself. The subject of your interview presentation will also vary. You might be asked to present on an aspect of your own life, such as a hobby, or you might be required to present on a current affairs topic. Alternatively, you might be asked to do a presentation that reflects the work you would do in the role you're applying for. For example, if you were going for a job in advertising, your presentation might focus on pitching to a client for an advertising contract.

Preparing for your presentation

The actual delivery of a presentation is only one part of the process. Let's start off by looking at the initial planning, preparation and practice you'll also need to do.

Once you've been tasked with giving a presentation, begin the process by answering the following three questions to help you to identify how to approach it.

What exactly is the presentation aiming to do?

Think about what you need your audience to take away from your presentation. Are you primarily trying to inform them or persuade them? In the context of an interview presentation, are you seeking to give your interviewers the necessary information on a subject, or are you aiming to, for example, sell them something? Your principal aim in an interview presentation is to convince the employer that you are an excellent candidate with all the requisite skills, but you also need to fulfil the specific presentation remit you have been given.

Who is your audience?

In the workplace, your audience might be colleagues, clients or a conference delegation, and in each case the audience will have different priorities and interests. Having your audience at the forefront of your thinking from the start of your presentation planning will enable you to tailor it more effectively. If you are presenting to a client, for example, you should aim to factor in their organization's style as well as their specific business requirements. For interview presentations, take the same approach as you would with a client, reflecting the organization's profile in your content. The specifics of the material you include will also be affected by your audience. From the information you can safely assume they know, to the jokes or real-life stories that will resonate with them.

How long do I have?

The third question you need to ask is a practical one: how much time do you have available? Your answer applies both to the length of your presentation and the time you have to prepare it. If you haven't been given a fixed period in which to prepare, be guided by the length of your presentation (ie 20-minute presentations obviously require longer than 5-minute ones), as well as the time you have in which to prepare.

Having defined the basic parameters of your presentation, you can now think about your preparation strategy. Start by dividing the length of time you have to prepare into three parts: content research and planning; putting your presentation together; and pre-presentation prep ie practising your presentation and sorting out practicalities.

A rough time ratio worth following for each part is:

- research and planning: 40 per cent;
- putting your presentation together: 40 per cent;
- practice and practicalities: 20 per cent.

This approximate guideline for how long to spend on each part of your presentation preparation can be applied whether you have a week or an hour to prepare.

Planning the content

When it comes to planning the content of your presentation, work out what background research is required – something that will vary considerably. If you are asked to present on your hobbies for an interview presentation, you will need little if any research time, in contrast to the research required if you are asked to present on an industry-related topic.

Gathering your material

Whether gathering your presentation material entails background research or simply drawing from your own experience, the next step is to identify and extract the most pertinent content. Let's say you are tasked with pre-senting on your final year dissertation: you won't be able to cover every as-pect of your project so will need to work out which key points would make for the most coherent and powerful presentation. Whether you want to and have time to write your presentation out in full or not, keep in mind the spoken word per minute equation as a guide to how much material to use: approximately 130–150 words per minute. Having a rough idea of whether your presentation should be the equivalent of 500 or 5,000 words will help you to work out the amount of detail you can go into, as well as the number of key points you can include.

Putting your presentation together

Once you've identified the best material to use, the next step is to put the presentation itself together. It can be helpful to begin by breaking your pres-entation down into a three-point structure: the opening, the main body and the conclusion.

Let's now look at what to put into each of these three sections.

Opening

In the opening section of your presentation you want to engage your audi-ence by capturing their attention, outline the purpose of your presentation, and briefly summarize what you will be covering.

When you are working out a captivating opening line, remember to tailor it to your audience: what is this particular group or person going to be interested in? Consider using jokes, powerful stories or hard-hitting questions, devices often used in public speaking to connect with an audience. It's worth keeping in mind that all of your opening section will make a difference to whether you succeed in capturing your audience's attention – it's not enough to just have a good opening line. From how punchily you define the purpose of your presentation to how interesting the summary of your presentation sounds, those first few minutes of content are worth paying particular attention to.

Main body

The main body of your presentation is where the bulk of the material you plan to cover will feature. This section forms the platform for your key points: aim to present them in the clearest way possible, carefully editing what goes into the final version of your presentation. As you refine what you'll talk about, you will likely decide to lose or gain material to ensure coherency or to clarify where necessary. When you're planning your main points, keep the spoken word per minute ratio in mind. Think of each of your points as mini presentations in their own right, set out in a coherent sequence. After making each key point, it can be effective to sum it up in a short concluding line for emphasis.

Conclusion

The final part of your presentation, like your opening, plays a pivotal role in whether your audience feels engaged. Strong closing remarks will leave a powerful impression, whereas a limp and inconclusive trailing off can disproportionately undermine an otherwise impressive presentation.

Signpost the final section of your presentation by mentioning that it is about to finish, then reiterate your central message and briefly summarize your conclusion. You want to ensure you don't finish abruptly, but instead build up to your ending. It's also worth considering deploying a memorable closing line, similar in effect to a strong opener, be it a challenging question, moving story or last laugh.

Preparing your presentation props

Once you've prepared your content, work out what presentation aids you need. The most likely 'props' you'll use are slides and notes to present from, but you may also use products for a sales pitch, or a whiteboard or equivalent for drawing diagrams or jotting down keywords. Slides, often in the form of PowerPoint, are only worth using if they add their own value. Used effectively, slides can illustrate and enhance the points you are making, and they can be essential for specific purposes such as presenting a chart, photograph or map. A poor use of slides, on the other hand, is when you simply write out and put up what you're saying. This is distracting for the audience and risks losing their attention, not least because they will often have read what you're going to say before you've said it. Any writing you have on your slides should be in short-hand and bullet points, rather than in full prose. Also ensure that the text you use isn't too small to read, there isn't too much text and that you have carefully proofread it.

The notes you use to present with will also make a difference to how successful your delivery is. In Chapter 6, when talking about public speaking generally, we discussed writing out a full version of what you will be delivering to then boil this down into a bullet point outline of your key messages. Again, where possible, it is advisable to use the bullet point version of your presentation as your main presenting tool. Reading your presentation off a long-hand script can take the dynamism out of how you present and make for a more passive audience.

Practice and practicalities

This final stage of presentation preparation might seem like an optional extra but is essential. Whether you have 10 minutes or 24 hours to do so, practising your presentation and sorting out any practicalities involved will make a significant difference.

Practise

Rehearse your presentation in front of others if you have the opportunity, asking them to pay attention to your eye contact and posture/body language, as well as whether you keep to time, speak clearly and at a good pace. If you have a very short time to prepare, for example at an assessment centre, run through your presentation in your head, keeping the points from pace to posture in mind. However much or little notice you have, also try to predict questions you might be asked and practise the answers you would give. If you are rehearsing your presentation in front of someone, see if they can think of questions to ask you at the end.

Plan the practicalities

Organize all your props and find out all the information you need to set up for your presentation, from where you will be presenting to the facilities available, such as whether you need to bring your own laptop for slides. Where possible, aim to set yourself up to present at least 10 minutes before you are due to start.

Presenting

One of the biggest worries for presenters is that nervousness will prevent them from presenting well. Being fully prepared on every aspect, from what you will say to knowing how to upload your slides, is the best way to calm your nerves and help you deliver your presentation successfully. Yes, you probably will feel nervous, but having everything you need in place will make nervousness far less likely to impede the quality of your presentation.

Here are some basic principles to apply to help ensure an effective delivery:

- **Keep your eye on the time.** Bring an easy to read watch in case there isn't a clock in sight, and check how you are doing time-wise at regular intervals. It's also a good idea to know roughly where you should be in your presentation, half-way and three-quarters of the way through your time slot – work this out in your practice runs.

- **Look around.** Especially when you're nervous, it can be tempting to present to one person: as well as being unnerving for the target, you are effectively ignoring everyone else. Instead, make a point of shifting your eye contact to different members of the audience.

- **Announce a questions slot.** Make it clear at the start of your presentation that questions will be taken at the end. Allowing questions mid-presentation can throw you, plus you may well answer questions posed midway at a later stage.

- **Pace yourself.** Consciously slow yourself down so that you don't rush through your presentation.

- **Pause.** Well-placed pauses, for example after finishing a main point, can be very effective in getting your audience to listen. They will also help you to catch your breath and think ahead, aiding the flow of your presentation.

- **Smile.** Smiling (when appropriate, rather than like a Cheshire cat) will help to relax you by warming up your audience.

- **Stay put.** At the end of the presentation remember to stay where you are so that you can take questions.

- **Bring your own water.** Bring a small bottle that you can easily stow away nearby, in case water isn't provided.

What to do when things go wrong

A presentation is ultimately a live performance, and it is therefore inevitable that things will sometimes go wrong. Preparing yourself for potential problems will help ensure that mishaps don't turn into show-stopping disasters.

What to do if:

- nerves get the better of you and you start to stumble. Stop – by taking a sip of water – steady yourself and continue. Pausing for water is a good way to get yourself back on track without anyone noticing;

- you lose your place. Stop and take time to find your place on your bullet point outline. A common mistake is to decide to skip a section or end your presentation abruptly if you lose your way. This is a risky strategy as you will lose content and can end up finishing too soon and/or failing to conclude your presentation;

- you are only halfway through and have used up all your time. If you have prepared properly, this is unlikely to happen as you'll have made sure your content fits within the timeframe and checked this by doing a timed practice. However, if you do run out of time, or are asked to finish earlier than expected, move onto your conclusion. This will allow you to cover any key points you have not yet got to and will also enable you to round off the presentation;

- your equipment (eg laptop) fails. Always have a back-up plan for presenting without any equipment. Bring printouts of all your slides and also have an extra electronic copy of your slides to hand, for example, emailed to yourself;

- you by mistake miss out a fundamental point. Finish the point you are on and introduce the missed point. It's fine to be honest and tell your audience that you want to bring in something you had intended to earlier. Rather than coming across as chaotic, reacting spontaneously in your presentation can help to keep your audience engaged.

What I found useful:

'Take a breath! Short pauses in a presentation can be very effective. They not only give you time to think about what you're saying, pausing allows your words to be properly heard and can also convey a sense of confidence.'

What I wish I'd known:

'Now I've been around the block a bit, I can see that the people you present to are an asset rather than something to be feared. Keep in mind the fact that your audience is generally not out to get you. They want to like you, and they're usually open to being informed and enlightened by you.'

D.G. (Filmmaker)

Exercise

Imagine that you've been tasked with doing a five-minute presentation about the street you live on, in an hour's time. How would you set about it and what would you cover? Break your thoughts down into the steps discussed in this chapter and sketch out a plan for what you would do for each stage. Finally, come up with a few questions that you could be asked on the topic.

19
Getting an offer

Getting a job offer doesn't mean accepting a job offer: it means deciding whether the job will work for *you*.

When you're starting out in your career, it's easy to get into the mindset that any job offer should simply be seized. Yet even job offers that you're sure you want require careful consideration. From weighing up all your options to clarifying or improving the terms of the offer, setting yourself up successfully involves a certain level of due diligence. Ultimately, your aim should be to make an informed decision based on whether a job offer will support your career aspirations, as well as the lifestyle you want.

In this chapter we'll look at how offers are made and what details to expect, as well as how to respond to an offer. We'll also cover examples of additional information you can request, how to try and negotiate an offer, and the types of questions you will need to consider in order to make the right decision.

The offer process

It is not uncommon to be offered a job at the end of an interview, or to receive a telephone call soon after an interview to inform you about an employer's decision. You should never, however, feel that you have to make a decision about whether to take a job on the spot. Regardless of the context, a verbal offer should always be followed up in writing, giving you the opportunity to fully consider the offer and look through the specific details. Even if you are certain that you do want the job, it is important to take some time to go through what you're being offered and, if necessary, to clarify any details. With this in mind, a suitable response to a verbal offer is to thank the employer for the opportunity and say that you will let them know if you have any questions when you receive the offer in writing. In the (highly) unlikely event that you aren't offered a job in writing, you *must* request a written offer before you accept the job, in order to have the detail and guarantees you need.

Offer letters

An offer in writing will often come in an email, although some organizations will post their offers. The basic information the offer letter will generally include is as follows:

- the job title;
- the salary;
- the contract length (for example, one year or permanent and full- or part-time);
- the hours;
- the annual leave entitlement;
- the organization's pension contribution arrangements (all employers are now obliged to offer a pension scheme);
- the starting date (for example, if agreed during the interview, or advertised as the mandatory starting date) or a proposed starting date.

In some cases the offer letter may also include details such as:

- the line manager the role reports to;
- any employee benefits (for example, private health insurance or a company car);
- working arrangements (for example, where you will be based if there are multiple locations, flexible hours and home working);
- any bonus schemes;
- reference to the organization's general terms of employment document – this is often enclosed or attached.

Your offer letter will also include details of the conditions of employment. These will generally have been advertised within the role description for the job, as well as discussed within the interviewing stage, so are unlikely to come as surprises. The most common condition for a job offer is satisfactory references, so if your references were not taken up during the application process, your offer letter may say that the offer is subject to satisfactory references. Other conditions might include Disclosure and Barring Service (DBS) clearance (criminal background checks often required by charities, for example), a medical assessment, or proof that you have the right to work in the UK.

Some job offers will also include details of a probation period that you will most likely have been made aware of during the application process. Usually between one and six months long, your employment will be subject to completing the probationary period satisfactorily.

Finally, an offer letter will usually make reference to a 'contract' of employment. In some cases, both parties will sign a separate contract document containing the details outlined in the offer, once you've accepted it. In some smaller organizations, however, the offer letter itself may be used in lieu of a contract, and agreeing to the offer in writing acts in the same way as signing a contract.

What to do when you receive a written offer

When you receive a job offer in writing, you don't have to reply with your decision immediately if you need some time to consider it. It's important, however, to acknowledge receipt of the offer as soon as you get it: not doing so risks appearing unprofessional or disinterested. We'll look at what you will need to consider when deciding whether to take a job shortly, but if you do want time to think about the decision, write back to the employer to say so. First thank the employer for the opportunity and then state a specific period within which you will get back to them. Although employers will generally be accommodating, you need to be realistic about how long a decision period is acceptable. As one HR director noted, one or two days is fine, but when the decision-making gets closer to a week it can look like the candidate is simply not very keen. If there is a particular reason you need time to make a decision, such as deciding between two jobs, or waiting to hear the outcome of another application, it can be helpful to mention this. Be careful how you word references to other job offers or applications, however, as you don't want it to sound like you are planning to take the offer only if you fail to get another.

Making a decision

During the application process for a job you will have done extensive research on the organization, as well as on what the role itself entails. By the point of the offer, you will therefore most likely be clear on how the job would fit your aims and expectations. If a job you are offered fits into your career plans, and you don't have the dilemma of another desirable offer to choose from, then your aim when looking through your offer letter should be to check that everything you require is included in it. If it is, you can then move on to accepting the job offer, discussed in the next section of the chapter.

If you are uncertain about whether or not to take up a job offer, however, the questions you'll need to address will likely relate to other job offers you have and/or the details and terms of the offer in hand.

> **TIP:** *If there is room for flexibility on your starting date for a job, indicated either in the application process or in the offer letter, go through the suggestions in the next chapter on what practicalities you might want to factor in.*

Identifying your options

If you have been through the selection process and are waiting to hear whether other job applications have been successful, one option is to contact employers you are waiting to hear from to alert them to your situation. There is no guarantee that they will be able or willing to give you a decision; however, if you are a preferred candidate, it will be in the employer's interests to let you know.

If you still have scheduled interviews to come, a level of speculation will be necessary. As well as working out whether you would prefer a job you have yet to interview for, you need to try to calculate your chances of getting it. Without doubt, attempting to predict your chances of getting a job, as well as whether you would prefer it when you have all the details, presents considerable risk.

If you do decide to take up a job offer when you still have interviews to come or employer decisions to hear back on, make sure you inform the relevant people. As well as being a basic courtesy that will allow employers to reorganize their plans, you may well find that you want to apply to work for them in the future, so it's important to keep good relations.

Your decision-making process may, however, be more straightforward: you have two or more job offers on the table. To decide, you need to ensure that you have all the necessary details to make an informed decision, from background research on each organization (including their values, priorities and outlook) and a good understanding of the day-to-day tasks in each role, to the specific terms of employment. In weighing up your job offers against each other, you need to work out which job will serve your career aspirations best.

Clarifications and additional information

Whether you have more than one job offer or not, never be afraid to ask the employer for more information. Pitched politely and enthusiastically, requests for more details will be taken by employers as a sign of due diligence and professionalism rather than disinterest or being difficult. It is, after all, in the employer's interests that you are clear about what you would be signing up to.

The main details of what the job entails and the terms of the contract will have been outlined in the job description and/or during the interviewing process. However, more detailed aspects of the day-to-day arrangements, for example how your role would be line managed, may not have been discussed. Or, for example, if training opportunities were mentioned in an interview, you might want to find out more details about what would be on offer. Alternatively, you might want to clarify something: if home working is an option the organization offers that you're interested in, how often do staff tend to work in the office? Understanding more about the role you have been offered, and in particular the practicalities, can be very useful in helping you to decide whether a job would suit you.

Negotiating a contract

The situation may arise where you would like to accept a job offer on the condition that you are able to negotiate on a term within the contract. The most commonly negotiated terms are salary, annual leave allowance, location and training opportunities.

Before you try to negotiate your contract, make sure that you are fully up to speed with how the terms compare within your industry, as well as the wider labour market. For example, if you are hoping to negotiate a higher salary, ensure that the salary you propose reflects industry norms. Equally, if you think the amount of annual leave you are being offered is too little, you need to find solid evidence that organizations of comparable size and work are offering more leave for comparable jobs.

The first rule to apply when going into negotiation on a contract is to ensure that the case you are putting forward is reasonable. The second rule to apply is to ensure that your approach is diplomatic. Entering a negotiation aggressively or unrealistically will simply undermine you. You are also more likely to be successful in achieving your aim by having a single clear point of negotiation, and by negotiating in person or over the phone, rather than via email.

Having done your research and established that what you are asking for is reasonable, email the employer to set up either a call or a meeting. Explain that you are very interested in taking the job but that you would like to discuss the offer – there is no need to state what you would like to negotiate on at this point.

When it comes to the call or meeting, start off positively by outlining why you would like the job and why you would relish the opportunity to work for the organization. Then introduce the term you would like to negotiate on. Your best approach is to be direct about exactly what you are seeking. As the most common point of negotiation in a contract is salary, let's look at how to go about negotiating a higher wage.

It's worth highlighting from the outset that when you are embarking on your career, bargaining power for negotiating salary is lower. This is unsurprising: your experience will be limited and you won't be bargaining from the position of a previous salary. As such, you need to embark on any salary negotiation cautiously. You *can* take a punt on trying to up a salary offer that is in line with the industry and your qualifications and experience; however, it is generally recommended that you only seek a higher starting salary if the offer you have been given is too low, either in relation to your skills and experience or in relation to industry standards. This note of caution takes us back to the importance of fully researching the industry and job market: you can supplement this by using one of the many online 'know your market value' salary calculators.

If you do decide to negotiate on salary, you should do the following:

- **Be specific.** Don't go into a negotiation simply wanting 'more'. Having identified the salary that would be appropriate for your CV, state the figure that you are seeking.

- **Back up your request.** Go into the negotiation with evidence to support your case, based on your skills, experience and examples of relevant successes; illustrate how these will add value to the organization.

The employer may give their final response to a salary negotiation during the discussion, and this may be a rejection of your proposed salary or a compromise. As such, it is a good idea to have decided what you are prepared to accept, before you enter the discussion. Whether your negotiation is accepted or not, and whether you accept the final offer, always make a point of thanking the employer for discussing your request.

Accepting an offer

When you have decided to accept an offer, the next step is to write to the employer to inform them. Some organizations will give you a standardized format for accepting an offer. For example, the employer may ask you to accept their offer by signing and sending back a statement at the bottom of the offer letter.

If you're not given such instructions, when writing to accept the offer, start by thanking the employer for the opportunity and expressing your eagerness to join the organization. The second part of the letter should confirm any relevant practicalities, including the following:

- **Your start date**. State that you look forward to starting on the agreed date.
- **Preparation**. End by asking the employer to let you know if there is anything you could usefully prepare before you start.

Keep in mind that when you accept the offer, it is not appropriate to include any queries. If you have any practical questions you need to discuss with the employer, such as moving the proposed start date, make sure you have done so via email or telephone prior to accepting the offer.

Turning down a job offer

You may want to apply to the organization in the future, and you may well come across the organization at industry events: with this and professionalism in mind, turn the opportunity down promptly and graciously, thanking the employer for the opportunity and their time.

Responding well to rejections

This chapter has focused on what to do if you are offered a job. It's easy to think that a *rejection* requires little thought and no action, but how you respond to a rejection matters. Again, you may apply to the organization in the future, or interact with them within the industry. But as well as building good networks and strong contacts, you need to get the most out of being turned down for a job.

However strong a candidate you are, everyone will experience job rejections across their career. There will be many reasons why you won't be suitable for a particular role – and indeed why a job wouldn't suit you. What's important is that you treat rejections as valuable learning experiences.

When you receive a letter of rejection, respond swiftly and politely, and say that you would be grateful for any feedback about your application (such as on skills to develop or experience you need to gain). If you are given feedback, make sure you thank the employer. Keep in mind that they have put time into doing so solely for your benefit.

Alongside any employer feedback you are given, it's also worth spending some time working out why *you* think you didn't get the job and whether there are any divergences between your assessment and the employer's. From recognizing that you applied to an organization that wasn't quite the right fit for your interests, to identifying experience or skills you need to build up, take stock of what you can and acknowledge that rejection presents an opportunity to improve your future applications.

What I found useful:

'I've found it very helpful to ask to meet the team I would be working with before accepting a job. It's a good way to get an insight into the dynamics of an organization and a feel for the working environment.'

What I wish I'd known:

'At the start of my career I was so desperate to get a job that I took one I didn't enjoy, as I didn't share the organization's values. As far as I was concerned, the organization thought I was capable of the job, so that was enough. But I should have thought twice about whether the organization would suit *me*.'

M.V. (Journal editor)

Exercise

How much do you know about your market value? You've been offered a job in your target industry that fits your qualifications and experience. What salary do you think would be fair? Now look up what salaries are being offered to candidates with your experience. How does your figure compare?

Part Five
Starting a job

20
Planning and preparation

The best way to counteract first-day jitters is to prepare everything you can.

Getting organized before you start your new job will make a big difference to how smoothly your first day, and first week, go, and to how calm you feel when you begin. Seemingly insignificant practicalities going wrong can be very distracting, so investing some time to sort out as much as possible before your job starts is very worthwhile.

In this chapter we'll look at what you can get organized and how you can prepare for starting your new job. We'll cover everything from basic logistics (such as your journey to work) to getting fully up to speed with what's happening in your industry. In most cases, you will likely have at least a week or two between being offered and accepting a role and your first day. But even if you have just a weekend before your first day at work, there will still be time to get well prepared.

Organizing the best start date

As we mentioned in the last chapter, something you will need to determine with your employer is the starting date for your new job. This might be agreed via email or phone or if you meet to negotiate the terms of a contract. Alternatively, a start date might have been discussed in your job interview. The decision will be based on a number of considerations, from when your employer would like you to start work, to any prior commitments you have – from booked holidays to finishing your studies or working a notice period for any part-time or casual work you are committed to.

Tie up loose ends

If you are given the opportunity to choose a starting date, do so on the basis of what you need to get done before you start. In terms of preparation for your first day, a couple of days is fine, although as we'll discuss, longer will allow you to take care of future practicalities, such as your work wardrobe and monthly budget. What you need to try to avoid is having to juggle tying up loose ends with your first few days or weeks in a new job. For example, if you have finished a taught course but have a project that is due in at a later date (this is often the case for a Master's degree), avoid planning to work on the project once you have started your new job. Equally, if you are committed to an evening job or weekend work that you cannot get out of immediately, it's highly advisable to finish that first. Rushing off to your project/bar job at the end of a long day in your new role will not only be a distraction, it risks weakening your performance: moonlighting on other work will inevitably put extra strain on you. In short, having another commitment on top of your new full-time job will be stressful, and you don't want to risk undermining first impressions because you are not able to give the job your all.

Fix up your accommodation

Along the same lines as finishing off any outstanding work, if you are moving accommodation for your new job, try to ensure that you have done this – and set yourself up in it – before you start. As well as having much less time and flexibility when you start working, being settled into your new home and being able to concentrate solely on adjusting to your new workplace is infinitely preferable. If you can't move until you've started your job, make sure you at least try to get property viewings out of the way. Some estate agents don't show properties at the weekend or after office hours, and you definitely don't want to have to ask for half a day off in your first couple of weeks at work.

Clearly, however, a key consideration for when you start your job will be money: you may need to start earning as soon as possible, and delaying your start date to get the timing exactly right may simply be a luxury you cannot afford. Nevertheless, it is worth doing whatever *is* possible to organize your start so that you can put your full concentration into your new job.

Make the most of your flexibility

As well as tying up any loose ends before you start your new role, if you have the time to do so, it's well worth getting routine appointments out of the way. It's easy to forget that once you begin your full-time job, an afternoon haircut or a mid-morning hygienist appointment suddenly becomes unfeasible. You'll be unlikely to want to book a day of precious holiday for such mundane activities, and every other employee will be competing for any rare working-hour friendly appointments!

It's also worth thinking about any necessary shopping you could usefully get out of the way, be it setting yourself up with an online weekly supermarket order, ordering a six-month supply of contact lenses or even getting a present for your relative's upcoming birthday. If you don't have much spare cash with which to sort life out until you get your first pay cheque, there's nevertheless groundwork you can get out of the way. As well as attending any free appointments and booking those rare Saturday appointments in advance, find the present you're going to buy so that all you need to do is buy it and pick it up once you've been paid.

Check your diary

It's definitely preferable not to book off holiday in your first few weeks of a new job – you don't want to appear uncommitted and you'll want to pace your use of annual leave across the year. However, go through the first couple of months following your start and check whether there are any dates you absolutely must take off; for example, for a weekday wedding or your graduation ceremony. The ideal would be to have already made your employer aware of these commitments when you accepted the job, but if you haven't, alert them to any unavoidable leave required on your first day.

Do you have a diary? Whether you use an old-school paper diary, an online calendar or your mobile phone, get into the habit of keeping good records of your commitments right away, if you haven't already. It's worth getting yourself a small paper diary as back up, whether you use an electronic version or not (for example, in case your device's battery dies or you lose your phone). As we discussed in Chapter 10, one of the qualities that employers value most in employees is good organization; knowing what you are doing, when, and avoiding scheduling conflicts is the foundation for ensuring you achieve this.

Organize your finances

Thinking back to our discussion on budgeting in Chapter 13, time you have before starting a new job is a good opportunity to take stock of your financial affairs. Once your contract details have been agreed, you will know exactly what your salary will be. Remember to subtract tax, pension contributions and student loan repayments when you calculate what will actually come into your bank account each month. Now you are clear on your new monthly income, it's a good chance to set your new budget and potential savings rate (see page 127 onwards for how to do this).

As well as working out your budget, before starting a new job is also a good time to review other aspects of your financial life. For example, look at any contracts you have: could you spend 15 minutes on the phone to try to get a better monthly mobile phone deal? Go through the savings suggestions in Chapter 13 and work out what expenditure you could adjust in your new working life. You won't be putting your new budget into practice until you start to earn, but it's worth doing the sums in advance.

On the subject of budgeting, now is also the time to double check that you will have enough money to cover your first month of outgoings when you start your job. When you are first paid will depend on where your start date falls within the organization's payroll period, so rather than banking on being paid soon after you start your job, have a solid back-up plan to cover your first few weeks of expenditure. Worrying about how you are going to pay your rent or afford to travel into work is a situation you really want to avoid when starting your job.

Preparing for the job

Read any guidance you were sent, undertake any tasks you were given and prepare any paperwork you were asked to bring. You will generally have been given instructions with details such as who to ask for when you arrive on your first day and what you need to bring with you. You will probably need to bring some form of documentation (if you haven't already done so in a prior meeting) such as a P45 or passport. Make sure your passport is in date as far ahead as possible, and also remember to bring along your bank details and National Insurance number for payroll.

Ahead of the last working day before your start, double check you don't have any unanswered practical questions. Make sure you are clear on the dress code and starting time, and if the organization has more than one site, that you know which one to go to.

If you haven't been given specific instructions on what to prepare for your new job, revisit the job description and ask yourself whether there are any aspects of the role you are nervous about. Does the prospect of using a particular piece of software, for example, worry you? Hands-on practice will help to boost your confidence, so if you have an hour to spare, spend some time getting familiar with what you may need to do. If you have a long interval between getting a job and starting it, it's also worth working on any skills gaps you have. Whether it's taking a short course or doing some voluntary work that gives you the opportunity to develop a skill, this is an excellent opportunity for upskilling.

Get up to speed with the organization

Before you start your new job, familiarize yourself as much as possible with the organization. From the organization's current priorities and recent developments to who works there, the website will be your primary source of information. Study the organization's latest projects and find out what you can about the staff, from their professional backgrounds to the focus of their work. Having a head start on putting names to faces will be useful when meeting everyone, and you will be able to join in the conversation much more easily if the organization's current work is familiar to you.

It's also a good idea to continue with your wider industry research: check out the latest industry news, via social media and relevant blogs, and look out for key discussion points. Also ensure you are up to speed with general current affairs, and if you don't already, get into the habit of reading or listening to at least the headlines each day. As we've discussed, being informed about what is going on in the world will help both your work itself and your social interactions in the workplace.

Practical preparation for your first week at work

Take a back-to-school approach to starting a new job and make a list of any new supplies you'll need. From a suitable work bag, to sorting out a travel pass or season ticket, work out what you have and what you need to buy.

Get your work wardrobe together

One of the best uses of any time you have before you start a new job is to organize a work wardrobe. Setting up a reliable work wardrobe gets rid of a daily headache: trying to find something suitable to wear each morning. You might not want to go as far as Mark Zuckerberg, who famously has multiples of the exact same outfit hanging ready to wear for each day, but it is definitely worth planning for five fail-safe outfits a week. If possible, aim for roughly five tops and two or three 'bottoms' (trousers/skirts, etc), so that you don't have to schedule a laundry session into your working week.

How smart your clothes need to look will vary considerably between workplaces, as well as industries. Silicon-Valley style, where trainers, jeans and t-shirts are normal office attire, is becoming more common, but on the whole, the dress code for offices tends to still be smart casual. Ties are often now optional for daily office life (common practice is to keep one in a drawer for important external meetings), but a shirt and smart trousers for men, and neat tops and smart trousers/skirts/dresses for women, are generally standard attire. If you are very clear that the dress code is jeans-and-trainers casual, you may not need to do much wardrobe planning, but nevertheless err on slightly smarter (for example, what you wore to your interview) for the first day. For more formal office wear, start planning as soon as possible. Begin by working out what you already have that is suitable, by putting together some outfits. Once you've identified gaps in your wardrobe, do some research on the best places to buy any new clothes you need. Don't leave this until the last minute or you'll risk forking out more when you have less time to look around and find the best value. If you haven't got the money to buy clothes before you start work, it's still worth doing the legwork to find what you need in advance, even if you then wait to buy any new items after you get paid.

TIP: *You need work shoes that you can actually walk in – and comfortably! It really is worth going for sensible rather than sensational shoes, so that you don't risk finding yourself hampered in any way. Also try to break in new shoes before you start – and take some plasters with you on your first day, just in case. Many a new employee has had to hobble home in agony because a stiff new pair of shoes has given them unexpected blisters.*

Organize your travel plans

The chances are that you will have a commute of some form to your new workplace. Start organizing your daily journey to work by finding the quickest and most reliable route, and calculate the door-to-door journey time. If you have time before your first day, try doing the journey one morning during rush hour. Organize your pass or season ticket in advance, and register it immediately in case you lose it. Whatever you do, don't wait until your first morning to join a lengthy queue to get your pass/ticket. If you're driving, find out where you'll be able to park and if you need to set up any parking permit arrangements.

Pack your bag

It's worth thinking about the bag that you'll use for work. While you definitely don't need to go out and buy something akin to a 1980s briefcase, do make sure you have a bag that is big enough to fit in what you need and that looks professional. Whether you go for a backpack or shoulder bag, just keep in mind that you might need to take a bag to meetings, and your tatty old gym sack may not add to the impression you are hoping to make.

The basics to have ready for your first day:

- your travel pass/season ticket;
- pen and notebook;
- any requested documents;
- wallet with some cash as well as cards;
- an umbrella;
- a small bottle of water;
- a second layer: office air conditioning can be freezing;
- a mug for tea/coffee, in case they aren't provided;
- lunch and some snacks.

And finally, relax. An important caveat to sorting things out before you start your new job is to get the balance right. Don't try to pack so much into a short amount of time that you begin your job frazzled. Your aim is to get organized precisely so that you can feel calm when you start. So, whether you have a couple of weeks or a couple of days, build in enough time to wind down at the end, to start your first day feeling fresh.

What I found useful:

'Research, research and research again. Don't stop researching the role and the organization just because you have got the job. Use their literature, their website and articles in order to familiarize yourself with the key people and their roles. An advance idea of the hierarchy helps enormously when trying to work out in those first few weeks, who you should go to for help. It also helps to inform the tasks or projects if you have a good grasp of the ethos of the organization and demonstrates a genuine interest that will be noted by your new colleagues.'

What I wish I'd known:

'Get into the right mindset. I wish that I had realized that those first few days in a role are more about how I was perceived as a person rather than my skill set to do the job. If your new co-workers and employers see that your attitude is right, they will forgive you the inevitable new girl/boy blunders. Experience has taught me that employers can be just as anxious as their new employees. Recruitment is a lengthy and expensive process, and they want to know that they have made the right choice. Give them that confidence by demonstrating your enthusiasm for what you face and your ability to pick yourself up and carry on with a positive outlook, even if it doesn't go quite right first time. It is amazing how quickly the right attitude will build their confidence in you and, as a result, their desire to provide support in order that you become a successful member of their team.'

A.R. (Senior marketing executive)

Exercise

If you were offered a job today, what general practicalities would you need to sort out before your first day? From renewing your passport or driving licence, to getting passport photos done for a railcard or registering an Oyster card, what could you get ahead with now? Make a list using the tips in this chapter.

21
Twenty questions about your first day answered

On the first day of a new job, many of the questions employees find themselves wanting to know the answers to are either practical or relate to problems that arise. As such, the questions answered in this chapter focus on navigating your way through frequently faced uncertainties and issues, from what to do if you're going to be late, to how to answer your office phone.

As well as looking at what to do in the moment, there are also things you can do to help you avoid quandaries happening in the first place. From familiarizing yourself with the organization as much as possible, to ensuring you ask any questions you have before you start, planning ahead can help you to sidestep quite a bit of uncertainty. Good practical preparation before your first day can also help to prevent unforeseen mishaps. Nevertheless, even the most prepared new employee will find that questions do arise, so we'll look at how to tackle some of the most common.

1 What can I do on my first day to help it go smoothly?

Setting yourself up well for your first day, both physically and mentally, is vital. This means really prioritizing a calm evening before your first day, so make sure you're not rushing around preparing up until the last minute. It's also important to have an early night before your new start and to leave yourself enough time in the morning to have a proper breakfast. You'll need energy to be alert and enthusiastic on your first day, both of which will be crucial for absorbing information and meeting new people.

Pay careful attention at all times on your first day: both in observing everything you can about how things function, from the dynamics between staff to the style of working, and in listening to any instructions or information you're given. Making the most of an initial session with your line manager, by asking any outstanding questions you have, is also very valuable. From clarifying the details of your day-to-day duties, to discussing how your performance will be measured and reviewed, establishing as much as you can right away will help you to hit the ground running.

Remember to take a pen and paper around with you. As well as instructions, you'll likely need to write down passwords, names and acronyms. Also jot down any dates for your diary, be they task deadlines, meetings or upcoming events that you should be aware of.

2 What time should I arrive?

First make sure you are clear about when your employer is expecting you to start. If they haven't given you a time, find out when they want you to arrive (don't simply assume that it will be their standard office start time). As we discussed earlier in the book, it is a good idea to plan your journey to your new office carefully, with extra time built in to allow for things to go wrong and in case you get lost. On top of this extra time, aim to get to your new workplace 10 minutes early, with a view to actually going in about 5 minutes before you are expected. Keep in mind that while you want to give yourself time to get to the workplace without hurrying, you don't in fact want to turn up at your office very early. The employer will want you to start at the time they have asked you to arrive, and they may not be ready for you – or even there – if you arrive a lot earlier.

3 What should I do if I get lost on the way?

You can avoid getting lost by planning your route in advance, and ideally by trying it out before your first day, as discussed in Chapter 20. Allowing contingency time, so that getting lost doesn't mean arriving late, is also essential. Best made plans can fail, however, so make sure you have the organization's telephone number saved into your phone, as well as your line manager's extension number where applicable. If it becomes clear that you are going to be late, ring your employer and leave a message if they don't pick up. If you don't speak to someone, it's also worth sending your line manager an email (so also keep their email address to hand) as they might pick this up first – for example, if they are still making their own way into the office.

4 Should I bring lunch?

Lunchtime can be a great opportunity to break the social ice with your new colleagues. A good first day trick is to stow a sandwich in your bag, but be prepared to be flexible. If it turns out that staff congregate in a communal area for lunch, join them with your sandwich – but if you are invited to go out to a local café to buy lunch, take up the opportunity to join them.

If lunch is not a social event in the office – it might instead be taken as an opportunity for people to catch up on personal or work emails and eat at their desk – follow their lead. In workplaces where lunch is a non-event, don't, however, be afraid to do your own thing after a few days, be it going out for a walk or meeting a friend.

5 What should I do if my work outfit looks out of place?

You may arrive and find that your clothes are less, or sometimes *more*, formal than what your colleagues are wearing, for example if you're wearing a suit and everyone else is wearing jeans and jumpers. However self-conscious you might feel, if your clothes are professional, the chances are no one will even notice. Your first day is all about familiarizing yourself with workplace behaviour, patterns and expectations, and navigating the dress code is part of this. Before you've actually seen the office style, it can be helpful to go for plain clothes in dark or muted colours, if you're worried about fitting in. If you do find yourself wearing a suit when no one else is, slipping off your jacket, and for men also your tie, can help you to feel more at ease.

6 What should I do if I don't understand a task I have been given?

Keep calm and go over the instructions you were given again, which you will have made sure to write down. If you still don't know what to do, find your line manager and explain specifically what you don't understand. If your line manager is busy, don't panic but look for other ways to occupy yourself. Was there a second task you were asked to complete? If so, make a start on that until your boss is free. Alternatively, go onto the organization's website or intranet and read up on a current relevant project. You can avoid having to keep checking whether your line manager is free by sending them an email explaining that you're stuck and want to have a word when they have a moment. When you do get the chance to talk to your line manager, mention what you spent your time doing instead: this will reassure them that you didn't just sit there doing nothing, and demonstrate your initiative.

7 What should I do if it's nearly the end of the day and I'm nowhere near finishing the task I was given?

Employers tend not to throw new staff in at the deep end on their first day, generally allowing them to ease into their work, so it is unlikely that you'll have a very tough deadline straightaway. It's nevertheless useful to clarify expectations when you're assigned any work: check with your line manager about how long they think it will take you to complete. Either way, at the end of the day talk your boss through what you have managed to achieve.

8 What should I do if I have nothing to do?

Not having *enough* to do on your first day is a more common problem than having too much. While some new employees' first day will be carefully structured with a full schedule of activity, others' may be less well organized. The first thing to do is to find your line manager and ask them what you should do – don't feel awkward, this is an oversight on their part and they will be glad you've made them aware of it. If your boss is tied up, ask colleagues whether there is anything you can help them with. If this fails, your fallback again is reading up on the organization's latest projects or seeking out industry-related material online that could be helpful to your work.

9 Should I offer to make other people tea or coffee?

Yes – as well as being friendly and polite, once again it's a chance to interact socially with your colleagues and to show that you're keen to be a part of the team. This is so much the case that for those of us who aren't particularly partial to hot drinks, it can actually be worth offering to make colleagues a hot drink for the sake of it. There's no need to go around the office asking everyone, offer to make a drink for anyone who happens to be within hearing distance of your desk or the kettle.

10 What should I do if nobody talks to me?

Don't take it personally. Your first day will generally be on a Monday, so for most people your arrival will simply be one of many things that happens at the busy start of the week. Take every opportunity to speak to people, however, by introducing yourself when a relevant moment arises. However preoccupied people are, they will appreciate your friendliness and willingness to engage. Simply introducing yourself is quick (you too, won't have time to spend the day socializing) and allows colleagues to strike up further conversation if they want to/have time.

11 I can't work out how to use a piece of software – what do I do?

Times like this are a good reminder of just how vital it is to be honest in job applications: if, for example, you claimed to be well versed in a programme you've actually never used, it's likely to come back to bite you. Your only option in this case is to be honest and hope that your employer doesn't recall the discrepancy on your CV. In all other circumstances, where you simply are having problems getting familiar with a new system or new software, again, just be honest and seek some help – either from your line manager or a colleague. Never put off asking for help: the quicker you are shown how to use a new programme or software, the quicker you'll be able to get on with your work. If no one is available, it's always worth seeing if you can find any helpful advice on the internet.

12 What should I do if the work I've been given is completely different from what I was told I would be doing?

First, keep in mind that it's your first day so it may well not be representative of what you will be doing more generally. Your employer may have decided to give you something simpler, or a task requiring less supervision, in order to ease you in. It's unlikely that you'll be given more challenging work than the expected standard on your first day. Nevertheless, if you are concerned, it's worth discussing what you will be doing in the future with your line manager. The best opportunity to raise the difference between the type of work you've been given and what you were expecting is at the end of your first day. Present your enquiry diplomatically, focusing on looking at your expected workload ahead, rather than your dissatisfaction so far.

13 How should I answer the office phone?

As simple a question as this sounds, it is one of the things new employees get most nervous about. From not knowing how to connect the call, if it's not just a case of picking it up, to being unsure about an appropriate opening line, answering the phone can be surprisingly nerve-wracking. Ask your line manager about using the office phone, including how to identify whether a call is internal or external, and how to dial out. It can also be worth checking to see if there is a telephone guide on the organization's intranet. Listen out for how your colleagues answer calls – this can be a good steer on the level of formality expected. The standard answering routine is a greeting followed by stating who is speaking, with the organization's name inserted after the greeting if the call is external, and often the team name inserted after the greeting if the call is internal.

14 What should I do if I feel unwell?

First and foremost, don't start your job if you're ill. The last thing you want to happen – you get ill just before you're about to start a new job – can unfortunately happen to anyone. Even though not going in on your first day might feel like a disaster, it isn't, and is unquestionably preferable to turning up ill. The employer will not want someone potentially infectious and certainly subpar in the office, and you don't want to start your job on the back foot because you feel awful, or find you have to leave part-way through the day. If you do get ill, contact your line manager promptly, explain that you are ill, and let them know that you'll keep them informed about your recovery. If you start to unexpectedly feel unwell during your first day, alert your line manager and explain that you need to leave.

15 Can I use my mobile or check my personal email/social media?

Keep your phone switched off and only check your personal email or social media at lunchtime. If your phone rings during lunch (keep it on vibrate when it's on) and you need to pick it up, take it outside the office and keep the call brief – don't lose any opportunities to interact with colleagues over lunch by being on the phone for ages.

16 Is it OK to ask when I'll be paid?

Absolutely. Although many organizations will run you through basic details such as the date the organization's payday falls on, either before you start or on the first day, you should definitely ask if they don't. There's nothing embarrassing about asking; it's a practicality you need to know to organize your finances. The best opportunity to enquire about payday is when you hand over your bank details for payroll.

17 When should I leave?

Avoid jumping out of your seat and dashing for the door the moment office hours end. Instead, when the working day officially finishes, find your line manager and ask them whether there is anything they would like you to do before you go. If your boss wants to have a chat about how your day has gone, fully engage with the conversation rather than standing with one foot in the doorway. Equally, if a colleague strikes up a conversation with you at the end of the day, make the most of the opportunity to get to know them. Avoid booking any evening commitments at the end of your first day so that you can be completely flexible and don't have to rush off.

18 Should I take any work home with me?

The simple answer is no – there's certainly no need to be working overtime on your first day, and it can get you into an unhelpful routine. However, if there is a recent report that would be useful background reading for your commute home, extra reading can help you to feel you're getting ahead.

19 I've been invited to after-work drinks but have an important family dinner – what should I do?

Stick to the principle of planning as little as possible into the evenings of your first week, where you can. You want to take up all the workplace social opportunities that arise when you start, both to get to know people and to show that you are keen to do so. Sometimes conflicting social commitments will be unavoidable, however. If this is the case, explain what time you have to be elsewhere and suggest you come along for a quick drink. It's worth highlighting that if you don't drink alcohol, that doesn't mean that after-work drinks aren't for you. Your aim is to get to know your colleagues, and whether you're drinking water or wine is irrelevant.

20 What should I do if I hated my first day?

Don't panic! Many an employee who has gone on to absolutely love their job didn't enjoy their first day. Being new, navigating an alien environment, building relationships from scratch and working out what you're supposed to be doing, can be tough. Things will get easier as you become more familiar with the organization, so keep that in mind and, remaining optimistic, reserve judgement until you get yourself established. If you are still very unhappy in your job after several weeks, identify exactly what the problem is and discuss it with your line manager. If things do not improve, you may need to consider looking for a new job.

What I found useful:

'First impressions count, so being dressed in something I felt was appropriate, but also comfortable, really helped me feel relaxed and be myself on the first day of my current role. On a super practical note, bringing both cash and card options for lunch was also helpful – you never know if people will go out to lunch, and if they do, what form of payment the café around the corner will take!'

What I wish I'd known:

'There often isn't a precise plan in place for what you will do on your first day. I now know that bringing work-relevant reading material with you is a great way to fill in time where necessary.'

G.T. (Scientist)

Exercise

Make a list of all the things you would need to know for your first day. Imagine waking up on the morning of your first day. What time will you need to wake up? What will you wear? Then take yourself through the rest of your first day in your imagination. How will you get to work? Who will you meet when you first arrive? What about lunch? Would you make a sandwich the night before, or buy one? Be as thorough as you can, and write down even the questions that feel obvious or trivial.

22

Making a good impression and building positive relationships

Making a good impression in the workplace can easily be misconstrued as being about the *first* impression you make. Yet what we're actually talking about is the reputation you build, achieved through your work rather than simply looking smart or keen when you first arrive. Making a good impression is therefore fundamentally important, with your professional reputation key to your progression in the workplace. Far from being about superficialities, the impression your colleagues have of you will play a central role in your future success in the organization.

Much of what we will be looking at in this chapter links closely to the characteristics employers want to see in the people they hire, from reliability to good organizational skills. There will also be overlap with the skills we discussed when we looked at effective communication in Chapter 6, be it email or body language. Ultimately, this chapter is about working as effectively as you can, both in terms of output and in terms of interactions. To achieve this, it's vital to keep in mind that making a good impression in the workplace is not just about impressing your boss/line manager – a common misconception. Positive impressions and strong reputations are built by taking everyone you work with into account and building good relationships right across the organization.

Habits to work by

The most effective foundation for building a good reputation is to put a set of basic habits into practice. Moving beyond the idea of simply having a professional attitude, these habits are about the actual implementation of professional behaviour. Day-to-day actions to adopt as part of your working routine, the habits that will serve you well in the workplace, boil down to practical ways to help you to embed efficiency and professionalism.

Take your time and others' seriously

As we've now discussed in a number of chapters, straightforward punctuality is a quality employers value very highly – yet tardiness continues to be a persistent complaint about recent graduate employees. The most effective way to get into the habit of being on time is to adopt a mentality in which you focus on the value of your working time and, crucially, that of other people's. Conceive of time as precious and something to be conserved rather than wasted.

A useful practical trick is to start by planning arrivals, to the office and to meetings, so that you are always five minutes early; then, shift your mindset to regarding five minutes early as being on time. Obviously, there will be times when things come up or go wrong and you will simply be late. That's ok. In keeping with taking your time and others' seriously, make a habit of letting whoever will be affected know as soon as you are aware that you'll be late. Apply this same principle to how you deliver work. Plan in contingency time whenever possible, and regularly check in on your progress. If meeting a deadline starts to look unrealistic, promptly make the relevant people aware that this is a likelihood.

> **TIP:** 'Be the first to arrive and the last to leave' is advice often given when starting a new job. There's no merit in presenteeism – being in the office for the sake of it – so smarter advice if office hours are fixed is not to gain a reputation for being the last to arrive and the first to leave.

Be dedicated to your job

The basic principle of dedication is to do your work as well as possible. In Chapter 10 we discussed the value of a strong work ethic to employers: striving to do your best is a key component.

In the simplest practical terms, doing your best requires you to do the following:

- **Optimize your productivity**. Make optimum use of your working hours and always put your full mind to your work. Maximizing your efficiency requires discipline: don't let your 10-minute coffee break regularly turn into a 30-minute one or allow yourself to have one eye on your personal email throughout the day. Fully productive working will allow you to work steadily, rather than having to ratchet up your output when deadlines loom. Keep in mind, however, that productivity also requires breaks: you also need to be disciplined about taking those regular 10-minute breathers and doing something completely different from your work at lunchtime – such as checking your personal emails.

- **Outlaw sloppiness**. Whether it's circulating a document you haven't proofread or failing to follow up on something you've agreed to, hold everything you do to a consistently high standard. Seemingly harmless sloppiness – not bothering to proof it because the document is only for internal use – *is* harmful, potentially giving you a reputation for carelessness.

The other facet of being a dedicated employee is having a sense of loyalty to the organization and a practical investment in it:

- **Keep abreast with what's going on throughout the organization**. The employee who has little interest or insight into the wider work of the organization is not invested in it.

- **Represent your organization well**. At external events, for example, this means looking out for the organization's interests and potential opportunities, and crucially, not bad-mouthing it. We'll all have complaints about some aspects of an organization we work for, but if you find yourself with nothing good to say about the organization, you're in the wrong job.

Implement systems to organize yourself

Like being on time, being organized is part of the essential infrastructure you need to work well. You also, of course, need to be organized to ensure good timekeeping. As with punctuality, we've discussed the importance of being organized in earlier chapters. However, because it is so crucial and because *dis*organization is such an irritant for employers, it's worth looking at how to embed habits for organizing yourself.

- **Plan out your workload, not only your meetings, breaking it down on a daily, weekly and monthly basis.** Using this schedule, at the start of each day, week and month go over what you have planned, making adjustments as required.

- **Don't try to remember things, write them down.** Whether it's meetings that need to get into your diary, or tasks to add to your to-do list, keep everything recorded or things will slip through the net.

- **Keep a tidy desk and a tidy desktop, by organizing and labelling your files and folders clearly.** Not only will it be easier to find things when you need them, if you're away from the office and someone needs to retrieve a document from you, they'll be able to find it and you won't be embarrassed.

- **Ensure your work is regularly and automatically backed up.** As well as making sure you save what you are doing as you work, back up your files on a regular basis.

- **Keep your work email well organized.** Don't let unread emails pile up; do create folders for emails you want to save, suitably labelled.

Self-motivate and self-reflect

As a music industry chief executive highlights, 'What employers really want are self-motivated people.' Set your own goals and targets, rather than just relying on your line manager to motivate you to perform well.

When you set your goals, give yourself regular deadlines for assessing your progress. It's not just beneficial to meet targets. Reflecting on what you need to do differently and what you need to learn when you don't meet them is also invaluable. Again, the employee who reflects on their work and takes action accordingly is a real asset to employers.

Set clear boundaries between your personal and professional life

Setting boundaries between your professional and personal life works both ways. To be effective in your job, you need to be focused on what you're doing rather than distracted by life outside it. But equally, when you have time off, be it in the evening, at the weekend or on a holiday, being distracted by work stops you fully switching off and recharging. As well as the importance of quality of life, to be fully productive when you are officially at work, downtime is essential.

A bad habit that is all too easy to get into with today's ever present electronic communication opportunities is not switching off your personal life at work and your work life at home. Strict boundaries are crucial, so that the lines don't blur into a scenario where you are never fully focused on either work or life outside it. In the office, keep your personal phone and email switched off during your working hours, saving personal emails/calls/texts for your lunch hour, unless you are dealing with an emergency. From an employer's perspective, using office hours for personal communications is clearly undesirable. However, the employee who is always finishing off their work after hours is also not necessarily giving the employer a positive impression. Rather than appearing dedicated to their work by putting in extra time, unless there is a specific reason for the arrangement, the employer may well see this as a sign that the employee is not up to the job and/or is managing their time badly. This comes back to productivity and careful time management: you need to get the most out of your (official) working hours.

Be ill when you're ill

Finally, be professional about being ill:

- **You are not ill if you have a hangover, you just drank too much.** Get into the habit of saving your partying for the weekend, right away.
- **Don't go to work if you _are_ ill.** Rather than being stoical and demonstrating commitment, it is actually inconsiderate to your co-workers and reveals a lack of judgement. If you are ill, let your line manager know promptly.

Building positive relationships

The impression you give and subsequent reputation you earn are formed by how you work and what you produce. The impression you make is also, however, tied to the quality of the relationships that you build with those you work with. And the two are inextricably linked: the quality of your work will suffer if you don't foster good relationships, just as the quality of your relationships will suffer if your work is poor.

Building a relationship with your boss

The idea that you need to build a relationship with your boss/line manager may sound counterintuitive. Surely the relationship is straightforward: you do what your boss tells you to do. However, building a good relationship with the person who oversees your work is essential, and regardless of your position – and their disposition – there will always be scope to do so. The reality of course is that it will be easier to build relationships with some line managers than others. But we don't generally get to choose our bosses, so it is worth implementing some basic behaviours that will help you build a positive relationship, whatever the circumstances.

First and foremost, talk to your boss – don't hide. A very common mistake is for employees to avoid talking to their boss unless their boss seeks them out. Limiting interactions like this can mean cementing a communication barrier between the employee and employer. It's worth noting that hiding from the boss often relates to a fear of scrutiny on the part of the employee. The employee who is maximizing their productivity and tracking their progress should, however, feel confident not fearful.

A great way to get on the front foot with your boss, as well as foster a more natural dialogue, is to get proactive by getting into the habit of seeking *them* out regularly and reporting on what you have been doing. A common grievance among employees is that their boss doesn't recognize their achievements. You can help guard against this scenario by making your line manager aware of what has gone well when you report to them. This isn't about blowing your own trumpet, it is about keeping your employer abreast of your activity in a way that is actually making their life easier. It's easy to forget that you will be only one of many aspects of your line manager's job, and if they are able to rely on you for updates on your progress, that's very helpful.

Building good relationships with your colleagues

Your 'colleagues' will encompass a whole range of people depending on where you work, but it's worth remembering that your colleagues are not only the staff on your team or those you interact with regularly. A useful rule for building good relationships in the workplace is to treat everyone who works there as someone you need to build a relationship with. However little interaction you have with the overall boss of your organization, or a part-time staff member who is rarely in the office, be informed about their role and be keen to engage with them when the opportunity arises.

So, what are the characteristics of a good colleague? Looking at surveys on this question, people's responses tend to include:

- does their job well and delivers good work;
- is reliable and dependable;
- is well organized;
- is knowledgeable;
- is dedicated to their work;
- is a good team player;
- is respectful;
- is trustworthy;
- is friendly and positive.

Significantly, the trait people appear to particularly value in a colleague is that he/she does their job well and produces good work. You'll also notice the overlap between the characteristics of a good colleague and the habits we've discussed that will help you to make a good impression, as well as those attributes we've discussed that employers look for. This overlap is a pertinent reminder of the consistency between the characteristics that will impress your boss and that make you a good co-worker.

Descriptions of 'bad' colleagues reinforce the above picture of good colleague characteristics and include being a poor worker, being unreliable, being dishonest, being unsupportive and not being collaborative. It's also worth noting a very practical aspect that is frequently cited: poor personal hygiene often features on the list of complaints about colleagues.

Being a good colleague and working well with others is again about more than having the right attitude – it's about actions. Here are a few pointers, many of them building on the basic characteristics of good teamwork:

- **Take an interest in your colleagues.** From making the effort to learn your colleagues' names swiftly, to engaging with them about their work and interests.

- **Ask for help.** You might feel that you should know how to do everything and that you are being a pain, but asking for and giving help are excellent ways to build workplace relationships. It goes without saying that all help should be acknowledged by showing appreciation.

- **Help and support others.** By helping others, you're not only doing something positive in its own right, you're fostering your own future support. When things go wrong for you, colleagues will be much more willing to help out when they have seen that you would do the same.

- **Be cautious about having romantic relationships within your organization.** Some organizations have rules specifically against staff relationships, and many would argue that this is for good reason. A key concern for employers is the danger that the relationship might end acrimoniously, with a detrimental impact on the workplace dynamic. Another concern, when the romance is still alive, is more commonly held by co-workers: that personal relationships can lead to favouritism or unfairness in the workplace. The risk for those in the relationship, therefore, is eliciting resentment.

- **Never get involved in office gossip.** Gossiping is often seen as a way to bond with colleagues but is invariably a mistake. Gossip is not only very unpleasant when you're the target, you're playing with fire by engaging in it. A good strategy to benefit from the bonding but without the negatives, is to shift the focus of the gossip. Whether you change the topic of conversation to the latest celebrity marriage, a hit new TV series or a recent political debate, it's always possible to find a way to chat sociably and compare notes that neither hurts someone nor risks entangling you in office politics.

What I found useful:

'I have always felt that admitting you are stuck on a problem adds to your credibility in the workplace and helps strengthen relationships with colleagues and bosses. I don't mean requesting support at each small hurdle, bombarding your line manager with questions 10 minutes after you have encountered an issue. But sometimes, when you have thought through a problem from many different angles, have checked emails and meeting notes to ensure you haven't missed something relevant, and have perhaps consulted with a trusted out-of-work friend, then you can present your problem to your boss and articulately explain your thought process. I found this helps build trust and respect within a team and avoids serious workplace errors.'

What I wish I'd known:

'That working long hours does not mean that you are working smart. Seeing someone arrive each morning with a cheerful disposition, buckets of energy and an arsenal of great ideas is far more attractive to bosses than the person they pass on the way in and out each day who looks exhausted and is joylessly working through their to-do list. Maintaining a happy, balanced lifestyle outside the office feeds your energy and creativity in the workplace.'

E.S. (Secondary school teacher)

Exercise

Think back to a boss you've had in a part-time paid role or voluntary role. Did you have a good relationship with them? If so, what do you think contributed to that? If you had a bad relationship with your boss, what do you think contributed to this? Is there anything you think your boss could have done differently that could have improved your relationship? Is there anything that you think you could have done differently that could have improved the relationship?

23
Planning your next move

Thinking about the stage when you're considering moving on from your first job will likely seem difficult to imagine at this point. Yet it's vital to look at your career through a long-term lens right from the start, to ensure that each step you take helps you to progress. This chapter focuses on when and how to think about moving on from your first role – from weighing up your future options within your current workplace, to finding a new job elsewhere and leaving an organization on good terms.

Keeping your career moving

Professional progression should be a priority in everything you do in the workplace. In practice, this means ensuring that you are continually developing as an employee, both by being sufficiently challenged and stimulated within each job you have, and by making timely moves to different roles and organizations in order to broaden your skills and experience.

As such, a central part of your professional development rests on being able to reflect on where you are and how you are progressing. In the last chapter we talked about the importance of being able to monitor, evaluate and motivate your own performance. This approach is central to tracking your progress and making decisions about your next best step.

With this in mind, each move, be it within an organization or out of it, should be carefully planned around where you've got to and your current situation, and what you want to achieve next.

Working out your next best move

Employers generally recommend staying with an organization for at least a year. In the words of an executive at a multinational that takes on large numbers of graduates, leaving a job after less than a year can look like either the organization wasn't happy with you, or that you lack staying power. From your perspective as an employee, you want to have something to show for your time in a job, and having less than a year to build a good record of work and strong relationships within the organization can be difficult to achieve.

The first-year anniversary of getting your first job is therefore a good time to work out what to do next. (It's worth adding here that if your first job is a graduate training scheme that lasts more than a year, it's advisable to complete it before thinking about making a move.) Should you stay as you are in your current role but seek better conditions or even a promotion, or move organization altogether? Importantly, your next best move will be very specific to your circumstances, and you don't want to fall into the trap of thinking you have to keep moving organization, simply for the sake of it. Keeping your career moving is about continual professional development rather than frequent 'fresh' starts. In your particular circumstances you might be best off moving to a new job in a new organization, or you might have more opportunities for progression at the organization you already work for. As such, the first thing you need to do is work out what your current organization can offer you in terms of career development and future opportunities.

Central to your calculations will be working out whether you are progressing within your present role. One of the main reasons that employees first consider leaving a job is because they feel they are no longer being stretched and/or that they are no longer growing professionally. As you hit the one-year mark, therefore, ask yourself some questions about the job you are in:

- Are you being given opportunities to develop?
- Are you learning new skills?
- Do you find your work stimulating?
- Are you being given training opportunities?
- Are you gaining the experience you need for your career development?
- Are you being given more responsibility?

Alongside these questions on professional development, you need to think about your working conditions:

- Are you being paid a fair salary?
- Is there a clear prospect of your salary increasing as your experience and responsibilities increase?

- Do you have a constructive relationship with your line manager?
- Do you have good relationships with your colleagues?
- Do you work in a positive environment?
- Is your commute to work satisfactory?
- Are you able to maintain a healthy work-life balance?

Your answers to these questions will help you to analyse your current status. Being badly managed, poorly paid, unhappy in a negative work environment or exhausted by a two-hour daily commute should be as important factors in your considerations as your opportunities for career development. If you arrive at the conclusion that you are currently in a strong position, with good progression opportunities and positive conditions, you will likely want to stay in your current role. Alternative scenarios could be that you would stay if you could renegotiate an aspect of your role, such as your salary; you would stay if you were offered a promotion, thereby changing your role; or that you would like to move organizations to improve progression opportunities and/or conditions or to change the type of work you do.

Negotiating within your current organization

A very common reason for considering moving on from a job is wanting a pay rise. In this situation, too few employees seek a rise within the organization they're working for and therefore feel compelled to look elsewhere. Don't make this mistake: work out what you think would be reasonable, pegging your calculations to similar roles within the sector, and arrange to speak to your line manager. Drawing on what we discussed in Chapter 19 about negotiating a higher salary, go into the meeting with reasons to justify your request and a specific figure. If you have carefully researched the salary that would be reasonable for your experience and skills, and you have worked well in your role so far, there is every reason to ask. Your request may be accepted, or it may be rejected, but if you don't ask you simply won't know what options you have. It's worth highlighting that if you have an annual appraisal – common practice for many organizations – this is an advisable point at which to raise your pay rise request.

If you would be interested in staying with your current organization given the chance to have greater responsibility within your role, or a promotion to a more senior job for which you have the necessary skills and experience, this is also something to raise with your line manager. Again, asking is imperative, and as long as your case is strong and draws on a good track record, there is no reason not to.

External options

Changes to personal circumstances (such as relocating) aside, common reasons for external options becoming a focus include: your requests for changes to your role are not accommodated; there is no scope for progression in your current organization; you want to leave the organization; you want a different type of job; you want to work in a different industry; a better job comes up elsewhere (with 'better' potentially referring to a range of diverse factors).

Regardless of the background scenario, when looking at any new jobs you need to compare what is on offer with your current opportunities. We've mentioned that moving organizations for the sake of it is not a good idea, so you need to beware of a 'grass is greener' mentality. It's essential that you do your homework carefully to make a sound comparison between the opportunities and conditions you have in your present workplace and what is on offer elsewhere. It can be tempting to be swayed by the prospect of something 'new', but new in itself is not enough. A common trap here is to end up moving sideways: in other words, changing workplace but not progressing. This can be unhelpful career-wise, as you may find yourself needing to build up your experience and reputation in the organization before you are considered for promotion – meaning that you end up in a less good position than you were when you had a track record and experience in your previous organization.

It's also important to factor in working environments, however. A key reason people want to change jobs relates to how much they actually *enjoy* working at an organization. A very pragmatic reason for making a sideways move would be to leave a workplace you were miserable in. You can be making career progress and earning a good salary, but if you are unhappy in your job – for example, you don't like the culture, or you don't share the organization's values – that should be a very important consideration in your decision-making. While you should be wary about assuming that other organizations will offer a 'better' working environment, the quality of your daily interactions will affect your performance not just your happiness. Equally important is to recognize the value of a workplace environment you really enjoy: while you should avoid forfeiting career development, you may find you are prepared to settle for a lower salary, for example, to work somewhere you love.

Looking for a new job

You may find yourself in the situation where you've decided to leave your current organization, but you don't have a new job in sight. In other words, you're embarking on a job hunt. The same core principles will apply to job hunting in this scenario that we discussed in Chapter 9. However, a key difference is that you are already employed, and managing to continue to do your job well while you look for a new one is essential. As we'll discuss, leaving an organization *positively* matters for your future professional relationships, your references and your reputation. You do not want to end up being the employee who has to all intents and purposes already left while still sitting at their desk. The basic rules for job hunting on the job are:

- Never look for or apply for jobs while you're at work. This is not what you are being paid for.

- Continue to do your current job to the best of your ability.

- Avoid shouting from the rooftops that you're looking for a new job. You may lose out on opportunities, you will unsettle your colleagues and your employer will inevitably see you as being less committed to your job.

Leaving well

Whatever the circumstances of your departure, you want to ensure that you leave your job *well*. A positive departure is essential for the all-important three 'Rs': your workplace relationships, your references and your reputation.

Ultimately, leaving well comes down to efficient planning and fulfilling your responsibilities. It's also about having a smart mindset where you consciously avoid slamming the door behind you. Central to maintaining good relationships with the organization you're leaving is to treat your colleagues and employer well. This means being considerate and diplomatic in how you communicate your departure.

Bosses and references

Understandably, unless your contract is coming to an end, you may be reluctant to tell your boss that you're applying for another job. Keep in mind, therefore, that if you haven't asked your boss to be a referee, you should not list them as one on your application. Only in application processes where referees do not need to be named until an offer is made, should you seek a reference from your boss *after* you've secured a job offer ie at the point when you hand in your notice. In some application processes you will be explicitly asked whether you are happy for your referee to be contacted before a job offer is made.

Handing in your notice

People often feel nervous about telling their boss that they've got a new job. However, if you fulfil your commitments and accommodate the needs of the organization as far as possible, there should be no reason to feel awkward or disloyal (two common feelings in the situation).

First, arrange to meet your boss face-to-face to tell them that you're leaving. As well as being a basic courtesy, it is much easier to have a satisfactory discussion about what needs to happen next when the interaction is in person. When you meet, begin positively, for example, by outlining how much you've enjoyed working at the organization, and how you've valued their guidance and the opportunities you've been given. Showing appreciation is a diplomatic way to pave the way to announcing your departure, and it will also signal to your boss that this is what you're about to do.

Next, explain that you have been offered a job, naming the organization (openness is important), and give the starting date. Make sure that you have double checked your notice period before you hand in your notice and that your start date for the new job is in keeping with this timeframe.

Your boss's reaction to your departure will generally be very practical: for them, the priority will be ensuring that you complete any outstanding work, that they are able to recruit a replacement for you, and that you are able to complete a satisfactory handover. For this reason, it's worth keeping in mind that your employer will probably not be jumping for joy at your news. Take heart from the fact that the stronger an employee you have been, the more disappointed they'll be to see you go. Do also be prepared for a counter offer from your employer. Before you go into the meeting to hand in your notice, work out whether you would reconsider leaving the organization if your role or conditions were improved. If you would consider a counter offer, discuss the exact terms with your boss and ask for time to deliberate before making a decision. If you do decide to take the counter offer, contact the organization that has offered you a job immediately and explain the circumstances.

With the employer's practical concerns in mind, if a counter offer is neither offered nor accepted, the next step in the conversation is to set out how you will finish up remaining projects. This will require thought and planning before you meet with your boss. When the meeting ends, thank your boss again for the opportunities you have had at the organization. Follow up the meeting by putting your resignation in writing for your line manager.

A further note on notice periods. Organizations have notice periods for a reason: so that employees don't leave them in the lurch with uncompleted work and no time to recruit a replacement. As such, it is vital to honour your agreed notice period, which will generally be between one and three months. As well as being a contractual obligation, this is about keeping good relations with the organization and behaving professionally. For this reason, it's essential to make prospective employers aware of your notice period at the interview stage. There may be situations in which there is scope for negotiating how much notice is required, where it also suits the employer better, for example if you don't have enough work to do because your main project has finished.

Informing your colleagues

Having given in your notice to your boss, promptly tell your colleagues, starting with those with whom you work most closely. Again, express how much you have enjoyed working with them, and outline how you will manage your remaining work, particularly projects that will affect them.

It's important to demonstrate to your colleagues that just because you are leaving, you're not going to become a bad colleague while you work your notice period. This is about not simply biding your remaining time in the organization but continuing to be engaged in the work you are doing and invested in your workplace relationships. It's also worth putting yourself in your colleagues' shoes: they are not leaving, so giving them the impression that you can't wait to get out is inconsiderate.

> **TIP:** *Resist the temptation to tell your colleagues that you are leaving before you have told your boss. The news can easily get to your boss before you do, and hearing on the grapevine that you've got another job will not only make you seem unprofessional, it won't allow you to manage the situation as you would like to.*

When it comes to your last day, again, don't just dash for the door. Show your appreciation to your colleagues and employer – maybe bring in some treats and write some thoughtful thank-you cards – and if you're invited for leaving drinks, graciously accept. Once you've left, there is a lot of value in keeping a sense of loyalty to the organization – both for your own professional reputation and because you never know what opportunities might arise in the future. If you absolutely hated working at the organization, there is little benefit in broadcasting it. Instead move on, having identified what aspects of a workplace you now know to avoid. The same applies to not bad-mouthing past employers, line managers and colleagues.

> *What I found useful:*
>
> 'Use your networks to find out about jobs and organizations that might be a good fit for you, when you're thinking about moving on. My first job was as a teacher. A colleague of mine moved to a research and policy organization, and when I began looking for jobs in that space, I got in touch with her to talk about it. The company happened to be recruiting, I interviewed and got the job. I wouldn't have known the organization existed had I not contacted her!'
>
> *What I wish I'd known:*
>
> 'Find out as much as you can about your prospective new company before joining. Even if you're keen to move on from your first job, be patient and spend time finding out about the organizations you are interviewing for. Jobs and organizations can look very different from the outside, so use the interview or – even better – go for a coffee with a current employee at a prospective organization to do some (tactful) digging.'
>
> *W.M. (Education policy researcher)*

Exercise

Imagine that you have got your ideal first job. Think of what the exact role would look like and which organization you'd be working for. What do you envisage your plan being after a year in that role? What would you need to do to realize that plan?

INDEX

Note: Numbers and acronyms within main headings are filed as spelt out.